Praise for *Exploring t...*

I don't know of anyone better than Rebecca McLaughlin to take a book of the Bible and make it fun and accessible for kids without compromising any of its complexity or depth. Rebecca and her two daughters highlight the historical context, the structure, and the big-picture message in a way that will compel you to love God's Word, worship His Son, and join Him on His mission. *Exploring the Earliest Gospel* is a rich study that kids of all ages will benefit from—I highly recommend it!

COURTNEY DOCTOR
Coordinator of Women's Initiatives, The Gospel Coalition
Bible teacher and author of several Bible studies, including From Garden to Glory *and* In View of God's Mercies

Rebecca McLaughlin has given families a true treasure. With accessible, age appropriate questions along with fun facts, illustrations, and prayers, Rebecca leads kids into the gospel story of Jesus in Mark with beautiful practicality. Not only will young readers find the truths of the gospel set out for them, but they'll be sharpened in how to study the Bible for themselves. That's an incomparable gift in a truly beautiful package. Any family or Christian school should consider purchasing this resource a top priority for their kids.

ADAM GRIFFIN
Lead Pastor of Eastside Community Church in Dallas, TX; coauthor of Family Discipleship; *cohost of the* Family Discipleship Podcast

I'm a big fan of this project because it gives young minds an excellent opportunity for robust engagement with the Word of God. *Exploring the Earliest Gospel* is not only a great way for kids to explore the book of Mark—adults new to the Christian faith would also find this project to be an excellent primer. I was excited to learn something new about my favorite Bible character! Approaching this action-packed narrative as a play is genius, as is the inclusion of world history, fun facts, and relatable works like *Harry Potter* and *Frozen 2*. The authors anticipate things kids would want an explanation for (like the Aramaic phrases of Jesus' first language), and each day ends with prayer prompts to guide children in responding to the truth they engaged with.

What makes my heart sing the most about this Bible study is how Rebecca, Miranda, and Eliza highlighted Jesus in a way kids can relate to—a Savior who was rejected, faced peer pressure, and became a Hero who grew a kingdom family we ALL can belong to. Bravo!

DORENA WILLIAMSON
Bridgebuilder and bestselling author whose children's books include ColorFull, Crowned with Glory, *and* Brown Baby Jesus

Bible reading is one of the most important aspects in the life of the believer. However, passing this on to young Christians can prove challenging, which is why I'm so thankful for Rebecca's book *Exploring the Earliest Gospel*. This is an invaluable tool that can assist young believers in their understanding of God's Word. The depth and accessibility are excellent!

JOHN PERRITT
Author; Director of Resources for Reformed Youth Ministries; host of The Local Youth Worker *podcast; father of five*

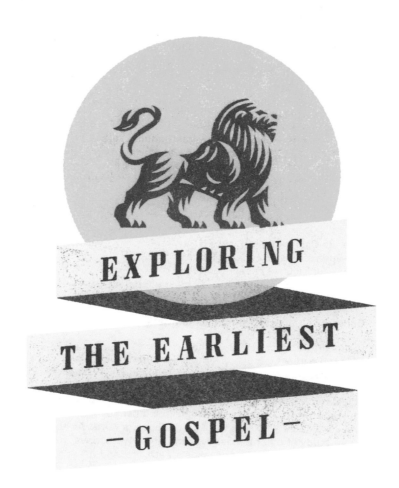

EXPLORING THE EARLIEST — GOSPEL —

A KIDS BIBLE STUDY ON

JESUS & HIS GOOD NEWS

REBECCA MCLAUGHLIN

WITH THE HELP OF MIRANDA AND ELIZA MCLAUGHLIN

MOODY PUBLISHERS

CHICAGO

Scriptures taken from the Holy Bible, New International Version®, NIV®. Copyright © 1973, 1978, 1984, 2011 by Biblica, Inc.™ Used by permission of Zondervan. All rights reserved worldwide. www.zondervan.com The "NIV" and "New International Version" are trademarks registered in the United States Patent and Trademark Office by Biblica, Inc.™

All emphasis in Scripture has been added.

Edited by Amanda Cleary Eastep
Cover design: Spencer Fuller, Faceout Studios
Interior design: Paul Nielsen, Faceout Studios
Cover illustration of lion copyright © 2022 by augustos/Shutterstock (1778868572). All rights reserved.

Library of Congress Cataloging-in-Publication Data

Names: McLaughlin, Rebecca, 1980- author.
Title: Exploring the earliest gospel : a kids Bible study on Jesus and his
   good news / Rebecca McLaughlin ; with Miranda and Eliza McLaughlin.
Description: 1st. | Chicago : Moody Publishers, [2023] | Includes
   bibliographical references and index. | Audience: Grades 4-6 | Summary:
   "In this kids' Bible study, Rebecca McLaughlin and her young daughters
   Miranda and Eliza guide your kids through the book of Mark. At its
   heart, this is a study of a person: Jesus. Through sixty-six days, your
   kids will gain more understanding of Jesus' death, life, and
   resurrection"-- Provided by publisher.
Identifiers: LCCN 2022033254 | ISBN 9780802428936 | ISBN 9780802474643
   (ebk)
Subjects: LCSH: Bible. Mark--Textbooks. | Bible. Mark--Juvenile literature.
Classification: LCC BS2586 .M35 2023 | DDC 226.3--dc23/eng/20220912
LC record available at https://lccn.loc.gov/2022033254

Printed by Versa Press in East Peoria, IL – December 2022

Originally delivered by fleets of horse-drawn wagons, the affordable paperbacks from D. L. Moody's publishing house resourced the church and served everyday people. Now, after more than 125 years of publishing and ministry, Moody Publishers' mission remains the same—even if our delivery systems have changed a bit. For more information on other books (and resources) created from a biblical perspective, go to www.moodypublishers.com or write to:

Moody Publishers
820 N. LaSalle Boulevard
Chicago, IL 60610

1 3 5 7 9 10 8 6 4 2

Printed in the United States of America

For Luke and Enna

CONTENTS

INTRODUCTION

Two months after the youngest member of our family was born, the oldest member of our family died. Granny Betty grew up in England during World War II, and when London was being bombed by German pilots every night, the children in London were sent away to live in the countryside. Granny Betty went to live with her aunt on a strange little island called the Isle of Man, where cats don't have tails. You might be thinking this sounds made up. But it's absolutely true!

If you have grandparents or great-grandparents, I bet they've told you stories from when they were young. They won't remember *everything* that happened years ago, but they'll remember all the most important things—like the day they started at a new school and got bullied, or the day they got married, or the day their first child was born. They'll also remember stories they were told, songs they learned, and things they memorized in high school.

The Gospels in our Bibles, known as Matthew, Mark, Luke, and John, were written when the people who saw Jesus live and teach and die and rise again were getting old. Like grandparents passing stories on to their children and grandchildren, they wanted the stories about Jesus to be remembered after they died. But while most stories told by grandparents are precious because of the family connection, the stories told by the eyewitnesses of Jesus' life mattered far beyond their local community. In fact, these stories about Jesus changed the world. So, how do we know they were remembered rightly?

Unlike our Granny Betty's stories from her childhood, the stories about Jesus that we find in the Gospels didn't depend on just one person's memory. Jesus had twelve official disciples—sometimes called "apostles"—and dozens of other disciples who followed Him wherever He went. It was their full-time job to be with Jesus and to memorize His sayings. The authors of the Gospels wanted to make sure that the stories of these first eyewitnesses of Jesus were remembered accurately.

Mark's gospel was the first one to be written. Mark was not himself an eyewitness, but he knew the apostle Peter, who was one of Jesus' closest friends. Mark's gospel is mostly based on Peter's memories, though it also points to other eyewitnesses. Peter was an "act first, think later" kind of guy, so Mark's gospel is an action-packed book. You may notice that Mark uses the word "immediately" a lot!

Experts think Mark's gospel was written between thirty-five and forty-five years after Jesus died—maybe even earlier. That might sound to us like a long time to remember something accurately. But Jesus' teaching changed people's lives. If your parents are between thirty-five and forty-five years old, try asking your grandparents to tell you about the day one of your parents was born. I bet they'll remember it like it was yesterday!

Mark wrote his gospel so that *everyone* could hear the good news about Jesus, and we've written this Bible study to help you read Mark's gospel for yourself. We've worked on it together, because we wanted to combine what author Rebecca has learned about Mark's gospel over the years with the perspectives of two people—Miranda (twelve) and Eliza (ten)—who are about your age. We also included feedback from a friend named Nathan Ridlehoover and his twelve-year-old son Jonah, because—like Mark's gospel—this is a book for both boys and girls.

When Rebecca was a kid, she visited the Isle of Man with Granny Betty. To get there, they had to fly on a small plane, so she saw the little island first from the air before she walked around it. We thought you'd find a bird's-eye view of Mark's gospel helpful too, so we've broken it up into six acts—a bit like a play is divided into acts—with a summary at the start of each.

We've also divided the book up into sixty-six days. That may sound like a weird number, but there are sixty-six books in the Bible, and studies in psychology have shown that it takes sixty-six days of doing something every day to really form a habit. So, in sixty-six days, you can work through Mark's gospel—either by yourself, or with your friends or family. And if you're new to reading the Bible, you can start a new habit of reading a bit of God's Word every day! We've based this study on the New International Version (known as the NIV), but there are many other good translations. In each, you'll find large numbers (1–16) at the beginning of each chapter of Mark, and small numbers breaking each chapter down into verses. Of course, these weren't in the original Mark wrote, but the whole Bible has been broken down like this to help us navigate each book—like street names and house numbers help us navigate in a city.

Don't worry if you miss days here and there. We try to read the Bible together as a family every day before bedtime, but some days we run out of time, or everyone's too tired, or our sin gets in the way and makes us not *want* to read God's Word. Don't be surprised if that happens to you too. Satan really hates it when people read the Bible, so he tries to distract us or tell us we've got better things to do. Sometimes, it feels like a fight to get the Bible open. But when we *do* read it, we're always glad we did.

There are two other ways in which Satan might try to trick you as you read God's Word. The first is that he might tempt you to feel superior to others on days you read the Bible. You'll see as you walk through Mark's gospel that Jesus' disciples sometimes had this problem. They wanted to look important, so they argued about which of them was the greatest. We can be tempted to think we're great for reading the Bible and to look down on others who don't read the Bible as often as we do. So, watch out for that. But the other way Satan tries to trick us is by making us feel really bad on days we don't manage to read the Bible. But Jesus doesn't love us any more on days we *do* read or less on days we *don't*! He knows we're sinners, and (as we'll see in Mark) He loves us so much that He died for us! Reading God's Word helps us see more of His love and character.

Throughout the study, we've added "Fun Facts" (or sometimes Not-So-Fun Facts) to help you understand what's going on. Here's one to get you started: Mark's gospel is written in Greek, which was the closest thing people had at that time to an international language. But Jesus Himself would have spoken another language called Aramaic—a bit like a lot of people in America today grow up in Spanish-speaking families, but also speak English. So, while almost all of Mark's gospel is written in Greek, we'll sometimes hear Jesus say things in Aramaic too.

Here's another fun fact: Jesus' life and teachings have had such an incredible impact on the world that we count our years from the approximate time of Jesus' birth. The years before Jesus are labeled "BC" for "Before Christ." The years after are labeled "AD," which is short for "Anno Domini"—the Latin term for "The year of our Lord." So, for example, 2023 means two thousand and twenty-three years after Jesus' birth! (You may also see this written as BCE "Before Common Era" or CE "Common Era" in some of your schoolbooks.)

When Granny Betty was living on the Isle of Man, everyone was worried that the German army would conquer and occupy Britain. But thanks to help from the United States, this didn't happen. The war ended when my granny was thirteen and she was able to move back to London. But when Jesus was born, God's people (the Jews) had been living under foreign rule for hundreds of years. They'd disobeyed God and been thrown out of their country. And even though they'd been allowed to return and rebuild God's temple, their country was ruled over by the Romans. They were waiting for God to rescue them. But God hadn't even sent a prophet for four hundred years. Until . . . well, that's where Mark's gospel starts the story. So, let's begin!

JESUS IS GOD'S

PROMISED KING

Mark doesn't mess around. He tells us straight up who the hero of his gospel is: Jesus the Messiah, the Son of God. "Messiah" is another word for Christ. They both mean God's anointed King, and in the first act of the story, Mark shows us that Jesus is God's King and His beloved Son.

As Jesus starts His ministry, we'll see He has the power to heal, to make us clean, and to forgive our sins. We'll see that Jesus is the doctor we all need and the "husband" we all want. (Trust us: we know that second one sure sounds odd, but it'll make more sense when we get there!)

At the end of Act 1, we'll see that Mark is telling us that Jesus is the King and Lord. But we'll soon find out that many people don't want Jesus as their king.

Act 1: Mark 1–2

—

**JESUS IS
GOD'S PROMISED
KING**

JESUS STEPS ONTO THE STAGE

In the first book of J. R. R. Tolkien's The Lord of the Rings series, a man named Boromir has a dream in which he sees a pale light lingering in the West and hears "a voice, remote but clear," which cries out with a poetic prophecy:

> "Seek for the Sword that was broken:
> In Imladris it dwells;
> There shall be counsels taken
> Stronger than Morgul-spells.
> There shall be shown a token
> That Doom is near at hand,
> For Isildur's Bane shall waken,
> And the Halfling forth shall stand."[1]

To understand this prophecy, you need to know the world of the story. The sword that was broken belonged to Isildur, the last king of the realm of Gondor. It is now owned by Aragorn, who has come to claim the throne. "Isildur's Bane" is the evil ring. "The Halfling" means the hobbit Frodo (one of the small, human-like people in Tolkien's world), who is carrying the ring. This prophecy points forward to the return of the king. Mark begins his gospel by quoting from two poetic prophecies from the Old Testament (Malachi 3:1 and Isaiah 40:3). Like the prophecy Boromir hears, the prophecies Mark quotes announce that something amazing is about to happen. But we need to understand the story of the Old Testament to understand the prophecy. Let's see what Mark says!

Read: Mark 1:1–13

In verse 1, what kind of news does Mark say he's telling us about Jesus?

What two titles of Jesus does Mark give us?

In the prophecy, God says He's sending someone (v. 2) to prepare the way for someone else (v. 3). Who is preparing the way for whom?

➡FUN FACT: The Greek word translated as "good news" is sometimes translated as "gospel." It means a special announcement from an emperor or king—for example, an announcement of a victory in battle. Kings in ancient Israel were anointed with oil, and our word "Messiah" comes from the Hebrew word for God's anointed King. Our word "Christ" comes from the Greek translation of "Messiah." So, when we call Jesus, "Jesus Christ," Christ is not His last name! It means "Jesus, God's anointed King." At the time when Mark was writing, "Son of God" was also a way of talking about God's King.

➡FUN FACT: In the Old Testament, "the LORD" means God.

In verses 4–8, Mark introduces a man named John the Baptist. Which part of the prophecy do you think describes John the Baptist?

➡FUN FACT: John's weird outfit in verse 6 would have reminded people of the great Old Testament prophet Elijah, who also wore a garment of hair and a belt of leather (2 Kings 1:8).

In verse 7, what does John the Baptist say about the person for whom he's preparing the way?

_____

_____

_____

What does John say that this person will do (v. 8)?

_____

_____

_____

In verse 9, who comes? Which character in the prophecy does He relate to?

_____

_____

_____

What happens when Jesus is baptized (vv. 10–11)?

_____

_____

_____

➥**FUN FACT:** The Bible teaches that the one true God who made all things exists in three persons: Father, Son, and Holy Spirit.

Which verses in this passage help us see that God is Father, Son, and Spirit?

Father: _____

Son: _____

Spirit: _____

In verses 12–13, where does the Spirit send Jesus and what happens to Him there?

_____

_____

_____

How does this passage help us to see how powerful and wonderful Jesus is?

_____

_____

_____

PRAY: Ask God to help you understand more of who Jesus is, to trust Him as your King, to worship Him as God, and to love Him as your Lord! You might pray something like this: "Dear Heavenly Father, please help me to recognize that Jesus really is Your Son who came to die for me. Thank You that Jesus is the King of all the universe. Please help me to trust Him with my life today. I want to worship Him and love Him, but I know I need Your help. Thank You that by Your Spirit You will always help me follow Jesus. In Jesus' name. Amen."

JESUS TURNS FISHERMEN INTO FISHERS OF MEN

How do you feel when people at school are picking teams? If you're athletic, you might feel excited. If you're not very good at sports, you might start feeling worried you'll get left till last. Or maybe you worry that you'll let your team down. In the passage you'll read today, Jesus is starting His mission and picking the first members of His team. We'll see later in Mark's gospel how everyone in this team lets Jesus down.

Read Mark 1:14–20

We learned in our first study that John the Baptist was pointing people to Jesus. In verse 14, what does Mark tell us has happened to John the Baptist?

_____

_____

_____

We'll find out later (in Mark 6:14–29) what happened to John the Baptist after that. Spoiler alert: it's not a happy ending! How does John's impris- onment help us think about the cost of following Jesus?

_____

_____

_____

➔FUN FACT: The word "repent" means to turn away from sin and back to God, like doing a U-turn on the road.

What is Jesus' message in verse 15?

_____

_____

_____

➡️**FUN FACT:** Jesus was announcing God's kingdom because He is God's promised King. The "good news" was His proclamation of victory and invitation to everyone to repent or switch sides before it was too late.

Who does Jesus see as He's walking by the Sea of Galilee (v. 16)?

_____

_____

_____

What does Jesus tell Simon and Andrew to do (v. 17)?

_____

_____

_____

What does Jesus tell Simon and Andrew He's going to send them to do (v. 18)?

_____

_____

_____

What do you think Jesus meant when He told these brothers that He'd send them out "to fish for people"?

_____

_____

_____

How could we "catch" people for Jesus' kingdom today?

_____

_____

_____

✦FUN FACT: Simon's other name is Peter. So, this is the guy whose memories Mark is mostly drawing from for his gospel!

What did Simon and Andrew do when Jesus called them (v. 18)?

_____

_____

_____

Which other fishermen brothers does Jesus call (v. 19)?

_____

_____

_____

How do James and John react when Jesus calls them (v. 20)?

_____

_____

_____

Why do you think both these pairs of brothers left their fishing boats and families "immediately" when Jesus called?

_____

_____

_____

How does this passage help us to see that Jesus cares about individual people, not just people in general?

 Thank God that He sent Jesus as the greatest King the world has ever known and that He includes His followers in His mission even today! Pray that God would help you to fish for people for His kingdom by sharing the good news about Jesus with your friends and family.

JESUS SHOWS HIS POWER TO HEAL

In the third book of Tolkien's The Lord of the Rings series, the strange-looking wanderer named Aragorn claims to be the rightful king of Gondor. A wise woman quotes an ancient saying: *the hands of the king are the hands of a healer*. "And so," she said, "the rightful king could ever be known."[2] In today's passage, Jesus announces His kingdom, gathers followers, and heals people suffering with spiritual and physical sicknesses.

Read Mark 1:21–34

Where did Jesus go on the Sabbath day, and what did He begin to do (v. 21)?

✦FUN FACT: A synagogue is a Jewish place of worship, and the Sabbath (Friday sundown to Saturday sundown) was the special day of rest and worship. The fourth of the famous Ten Commandments that God gives to His people in the Old Testament is to "Remember the Sabbath day by keeping it holy" (Exodus 20:8).

How did people react to Jesus' teaching (v. 22)?

How was He different from the teachers of the law (v. 22)?

_____

_____

_____

Who started shouting (v. 23)?

_____

_____

_____

☲✦FUN FACT: Okay, maybe this fact isn't so fun! But in the Gospels, Jesus often encounters people with evil or "impure" spirits. Another term for this would be "demon-possessed." These spirits all tend to have a similar reaction to Jesus.

What two questions did this evil spirit, speaking through the man, ask (v. 24)?

_____

_____

_____

☲✦FUN FACT: In Jesus' day, people didn't have last names in the same way we do, so sometimes they were known by their first name and where they came from. Jesus was often called "Jesus of Nazareth" because He had a common first name.

What did the demon-possessed man say about Jesus (v. 24)?

_____

_____

_____

What two things did Jesus say to the evil spirit?

_____

_____

_____

➡️*FUN FACT:* In the Gospels, Jesus often tells people to keep quiet about who He really is, because He isn't yet ready to reveal His true identity to everyone. He knows that when He does that He'll be killed. This has always been Jesus' plan, but He knows the right time for it. He also knows that people will misunderstand His mission when they hear that He is God's anointed King, so He keeps things quiet.

What did the impure spirit do on Jesus' command (v. 26)?

Why were the people amazed (v. 27)?

Where did Jesus go (v. 29)?

What was wrong with Simon Peter's mother-in-law (v. 30)?

What did Jesus do and how did the sick woman react (v. 31)?

➡✦FUN FACT: When Jesus heals people in the Gospels, they often want to serve or follow Him.

In verses 32–34, what things happen again that have already happened in this passage?

_____

_____

_____

 PRAY: Thank God that Jesus has the power both to teach us and to heal us. Thank Him that Jesus has control over physical and spiritual sickness. Pray for someone you know who is sick, that Jesus would heal them and that they'd respond like Simon's mother-in-law by serving Him!

JESUS SHOWS HIS POWER
TO MAKE CLEAN

In March 2021, our family had to quarantine. Two of us had tested positive for the COVID-19 virus, so we had to keep away from school and work and all our friends until we were considered no longer infectious. In Jesus' day, there was a skin disease called leprosy. It was a terrible disease, and people believed that if you touched someone with leprosy, you'd very likely get it too. So, lepers had to live away from everybody else. But in today's passage, we see Jesus has no problem touching lepers.

Read Mark 1:35–45

In verse 35, Jesus goes to a solitary place, which means a place where He could be alone. What did Jesus do there?

_____

_____

_____

People had just been flocking to Jesus for healing. What do you think we can learn from Jesus' choice to leave the crowd the next morning to pray?

_____

_____

_____

_____

What do Simon Peter and the other disciples do (v. 36)?

_____

_____

_____

What did they tell Jesus when they found Him (v. 37)?

_____

_____

_____

Why do you think everyone was looking for Jesus?

_____

_____

_____

What did Jesus say they should do and why (v. 38)?

_____

_____

_____

What two things did Jesus do as they traveled throughout Galilee (v. 39)?

_____

_____

_____

➵✦FUN FACT: In Jewish law, there were lots of things that could make you "unclean" and unable, for example, to participate in worship in the temple in Jerusalem. Having a skin disease like leprosy was one of the things that made you unclean in this way.

Who came to Jesus in verse 40?

_____

_____

What did this man with leprosy do and what did he say (v. 40)?

_____

_____

_____

How did Jesus feel (v. 41)?

_____

_____

_____

✦FUN FACT: There are a few places in the Gospels where we are not completely sure what the original text said. Your Bible might say that Jesus was indignant or that he was "filled with compassion," because some early copies of Mark's gospel say one and others say the other. This is one of a few places where experts aren't sure which is right. But if the original does say that Jesus was indignant (i.e., angry), He's clearly not angry with the man!

What amazing thing does Jesus do in verse 41?

_____

_____

_____

What happened to the man when Jesus touched him and said, "Be clean"?

_____

_____

_____

What did Jesus tell the man to do and not to do (v. 44)?

_____

_____

_____

≡✦*FUN FACT:* In Mark's gospel, Jesus often tells people He has healed to keep it quiet, just like He told the demon in verse 25 to be quiet.

In verse 44, instead of keeping quiet, the man went around telling everyone about Jesus. Why do you think he did this?

_____

_____

_____

What was the result of the man telling everyone in (v. 45)?

_____

_____

_____

PRAY: Thank Jesus for being so loving and for touching this sick man. Ask Him to help you see how loving He is and to bring all your problems to Him.

JESUS SHOWS HIS POWER
TO FORGIVE

Miranda (who just turned twelve) is famous in our family for asking, "Would you rather?" questions. Sometimes, they're questions about magical powers, like, "Would you rather be able to fly or to teleport?" Sometimes, she just asks, "If you could have a superpower, what would it be?" In our passage today, we'll see Jesus using two of His super-powers: the power to heal and the power to forgive sins. If we were picking one of those superpowers, we might pick the power to heal. After all, there are a lot of really sick people in the world, and it would be amazing to be able to heal them! But we'll see in Mark today which power Jesus thinks is more important.

Read: Mark 2:1–12

In verses 1–2, what happened when everyone found out that Jesus was home?

_____

_____

_____

What did the friends of the paralyzed man do in verses 3–4?

_____

_____

_____

What do you think they were hoping Jesus would do?

What does Jesus do instead in verse 5?

How do the teachers of the law react in verses 6–7?

↦**FUN FACT:** Okay. Again, it's not so fun. Sin hurts other people, but it is also an offense against God. So, only God has the right to forgive sins. That's why the teachers of the law are so shocked by Jesus' words. They think He is "blaspheming" (saying something bad and untrue about God) because Jesus is claiming He can do what only God can do.

How does Jesus respond to their complaint (vv. 8–9)?

How would you answer Jesus' question (v. 9)?

We might think it's easier to say, "Your sins are forgiven!" than "Get up and walk," because you can't see someone being forgiven, so you could say it had happened when it hadn't. But how does Jesus prove He has forgiven the man's sins in verses 10–12?

How does Jesus use His power in this story?

How did people respond in verse 12?

In our society, people spend a lot of money on doctors and medicine and hospitals—and physical healing is good! In fact, the world's first hospitals were started by Christians because they wanted sick people to have a place where they could be cared for. But what difference would it make in our society today if people believed that having your sins forgiven was even more important than physical healing?

For Jesus, it was easy to heal people. He just had to say the word. But as we read on in the gospel of Mark, we'll find that forgiving people's sins is much harder. It cost Jesus His life.

 PRAY: Thank Jesus for winning forgiveness for your sins by His death on the cross. Pray that when life is hard He would help you have faith in Him, like the paralyzed man's friends.

JESUS IS
THE DOCTOR WE NEED

In *The Fault in Our Stars* by John Green, a seventeen-year-old boy named Augustus doesn't realize he has cancer until it's too late for his life to be saved. If he'd known about the cancer earlier and gone to see a doctor, he could have been made well. But he didn't. In our passage today, we'll see some people who realize they are spiritually sick and go to Jesus the doctor for help, while others think they're well and don't seek His help.

Read Mark 2:13–17

In verse 13, where was Jesus and what was He doing?

_____

_____

_____

In verse 14, who did Jesus see and what was he doing?

_____

_____

_____

✦**FUN FACT:** Tax collectors were seen as bad people by other Jews because they worked for the Romans who ruled over the Jewish people. They also made people give them extra money and kept it for themselves. People hated tax collectors and thought of them as awful sinners.

What did Jesus say to Levi?

Why is it surprising that Jesus would call a tax collector?

How did Levi respond when Jesus called him?

What does this teach us about how we should respond to Jesus?

➔*FUN FACT:* Levi's other name was Matthew (see Matthew 9:9), and we think that he wrote Matthew's gospel!

In verse 15, Levi threw a party for Jesus. What kind of people was Jesus eating dinner with?

In verse 16, who complained about Jesus eating dinner with these people?

In verse 17, how does Jesus respond to the Pharisees?

⇒ **FUN FACT:** "Righteous" means being right with God. The Pharisees were extremely religious Jews. Most people would have seen them as super holy: the most righteous people in town! When we meet Pharisees in the Gospels, that's almost always how they see themselves. But we'll notice as Mark's gospel unfolds that the Pharisees hate Jesus and don't want Him to be king.

When Jesus said He didn't come for the righteous, but for sinners, which category do you think the Pharisees would have put themselves in?

Do you think Jesus thought the Pharisees were righteous or sinners?

Mark often tells his stories in an order to help us understand each story better. You may have noticed that this story about Levi connects with yesterday's story about Jesus healing the paralyzed man.

Who is sick in each passage?

Who is the doctor in each passage?

_____

_____

_____

Who criticizes Jesus in each passage?

_____

_____

_____

PRAY: According to the Bible, we're all desperately spiritually sick, and the only way we can be right with God is by coming to Jesus, the great doctor who can make us spiritually well. Ask Jesus to help you recognize that you are a sinner in need of His forgiveness.

JESUS IS THE HUSBAND
WE WANT

In the 1992 Disney film *Aladdin,* Aladdin and Princess Jasmine sing a song together called "A Whole New World" about how their love for each other has changed everything. Lots of stories make it sound like falling in love and getting married is the most important thing in the world. But in our passage today, we'll get a clue to something much more important than romantic love. If you're a boy, you might think it sounds strange to say that Jesus is the husband we all want. But it will make sense in the end!

Read Mark 2:18–22

In verse 18, what were John the Baptist's disciples and the Pharisees doing?

✦FUN FACT: Fasting means not eating for some time. In the Bible, people fast in order to focus on prayer or to express their sorrow about their situation or about their sin.

In verse 19, what does Jesus say when He's asked why His disciples don't fast?

✦FUN FACT: In the Old Testament, God is often pictured as a loving husband, and His people (the Israelites) as His wife. But their marriage doesn't work because God's people keep cheating on Him with other so-called gods.

How does this Old Testament picture help us understand what Jesus means when He says He is the bridegroom (which means the man at a wedding who is getting married)?

What do you think Jesus meant when He said the days are coming when the bridegroom will be taken away?

If marriage is meant to point to Jesus' love for His people, how does that help us understand why we need to stick with God's design for marriage as one man and one woman together for life?

➡ **FUN FACT:** In his letter to the church in Ephesus, the apostle Paul explains that Christian marriage is meant to copy Jesus' relationship with His people. Paul says that Christian husbands must love their wives like Jesus loved the church and gave Himself up for her (Ephesians 5:25). You might be thinking this sounds super weird. Jesus is one person, and the church is lots of people, male and female; so how can the church be Jesus' bride? This is a metaphor or word picture to help us understand how Jesus loves us, and the Bible is full of metaphors. For instance, when John the Baptist says that Jesus is "the Lamb of God," this doesn't mean that Jesus is *literally* a young sheep. John is pointing us to Jesus as the one who would be sacrificed for sin, like lambs were sacrificed.

People sometimes act like "falling in love" and getting married is the most important thing. But the Bible teaches that Jesus is the real bridegroom and we, together, are His bride. That means if we never get married, our lives as single people can be just as full and faithful to the Lord as if we had married. Do you ever worry about whether you'll get married? If you do, take a minute now to write down why you worry about that, and look back at your thoughts when it comes time to pray.

In verse 21, what does Jesus say will happen if you sew a piece of unshrunk (or new) cloth on an old piece of clothing?

In verse 22, what does Jesus say will happen if you put new wine into old wineskins?

In both examples, Jesus says that trying to fit something new into something old doesn't work. How does this help us think about Jesus' coming to earth as the start of something new?

PRAY: The older you get, the more you'll likely be tempted to believe that romantic love is the most important thing. Ask Jesus to help you believe that His love is better than any human love; and being in His family is better than falling in love and getting married.

JESUS IS THE KING
AND LORD

If you've ever read a children's Bible, you'll have read the story of David and Goliath. David was a shepherd who became the greatest king in the history of God's people. He's most known for his epic victory over a super-sized enemy of God's people named Goliath. But David wasn't perfect. In fact, he committed adultery and murder, so he had to do some serious repenting. But still, God's people looked back to King David as a hero, and God had promised David that his throne would be an everlasting one. In fact, there are many Old Testament prophecies about God's promised King—the Messiah—who would one day sit on David's throne and rule forevermore. Today, we'll get a hint from Jesus that He is that promised King.

Read Mark 2:23–28

In verse 23, what day is it, and what are Jesus and His disciples doing?

_____

_____

_____

✦*FUN FACT:* According to the Old Testament law, the Sabbath was a day to rest and to worship God. People weren't allowed to work on the Sabbath, so the Pharisees complain that Jesus and His disciples are doing something that could be thought of as work.

Who does Jesus reference when He responds to the Pharisees in verses 25–26?

_____

_____

_____

Where does Jesus say King David went when he was hungry?

What does Jesus say King David did in the house of God?

→FUN FACT: Here, the Pharisees witness Jesus doing whatever King David had the right to do. Jesus *did* have that right. But to the Pharisees, this seemed outrageous—like if you said, "Well, the President can go into the White House and take what he wants, so I can too." Jesus is simply being who He is—God's anointed King, with the same rights as King David.

In verse 27, what does Jesus say about the Sabbath?

In verse 28, what does Jesus say about Himself?

→FUN FACT: This would have sounded even *more* outrageous to the Pharisees. God Himself is Lord of the Sabbath!

How does this story help us see who Jesus is?

PRAY:
Praise Jesus that He is a better, greater, and stronger King than David ever was. Praise Him that He is the rightful Lord of everyone, and ask Him to help you live with Him as your King today!

Well done for working through the first act of Mark's gospel! We've covered lots of ground and learned a lot about King Jesus. In the next act, we'll see Him starting His new kingdom family.

JESUS STARTS

HIS KINGDOM

FAMILY

Mark's second act begins with Jesus being rejected by the religious and political leaders, but also being followed by great crowds. We see Jesus calling His disciples and appointing some of them to be His twelve apostles. His family thinks He's crazy! But Jesus says He's starting a new family of those who do the will of God.

Jesus tells a story with a meaning, also known as a parable, about a farmer sowing seed on different kinds of ground. He tells this story to show that some people will accept God's Word while others won't. He tells more stories about God's kingdom, and then He shows His terrifying power over nature and over demons!

To grow His family more, Jesus heals two daughters: a synagogue ruler's twelve-year-old daughter who has died, and a woman who has been bleeding for twelve years, whom Jesus calls His daughter.

Act 1: Mark 1–2

JESUS IS GOD'S PROMISED KING

Act 2: Mark 3–5

JESUS STARTS HIS KINGDOM FAMILY

DAY
9

JESUS IS REJECTED BY THE RELIGIOUS LEADERS

In C. S. Lewis's *The Lion, the Witch and the Wardrobe*, Peter, Susan, Edmund, and Lucy have been evacuated from London because of the war—just like Granny Betty was in real life! The children go to live in a large house in the country, which is owned by a professor and run by a housekeeper named Mrs. Macready. Mrs. Macready is very strict and adds a lot of rules, as if they're what the professor wants. But actually, they're not. Throughout Mark's gospel, the Pharisees try to get Jesus in trouble for breaking God's rules, when actually, Jesus is not. Our passage today is one example.

Read Mark 3:1–12

In verse 1, who is in the synagogue along with Jesus?

In verse 2, what were some of the Pharisees looking for?

What does Jesus do in verse 3?

What question does Jesus ask in verse 4?

_____

_____

_____

What do you think the right answer to Jesus' question is?

_____

_____

_____

Why do you think the Pharisees didn't answer?

_____

_____

_____

In verse 5, how did Jesus feel and why did He feel that way?

_____

_____

_____

➣✦FUN FACT: In the Gospels, we often find that Jesus is able to see what's really going on in people's hearts. He can see into our hearts today as well!

What did Jesus do in verse 5, and what happened?

_____

_____

_____

How do you think the man felt when his hand was made well?

In verse 6, how did the Pharisees react when Jesus heals the man?

Why is it strange that the Pharisees would plot together with the Herodians?

How does the reaction of the Pharisees show their real answer to Jesus' question in verse 4?

In verses 8–10, we see a very different reaction to Jesus from the response of the Pharisees. How are people from the surrounding areas and especially sick people reacting to Jesus?

How does the reaction of the impure spirits in verse 11 echo what God said to Jesus at His baptism in our first study (Mark 1:11)?

_____

_____

_____

➡✦**FUN FACT:** Throughout Mark's gospel, we'll see that Jesus is opposed and rejected by some and welcomed by others. He's the true King God always promised He would send. But many people don't want Him to be King and don't think they need Him. The same is true today.

 Ask Jesus to help you see the parts of your heart that are stubborn and resisting Jesus' loving rule. If there are kids in your school or neighborhood who seem like they are out to get you, thank God that Jesus knows just what it feels like. Ask Him to help you trust Him when you're feeling under attack and not to just fight back.

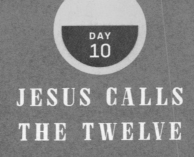

JESUS CALLS THE TWELVE

In J. R. R. Tolkien's *The Fellowship of the Ring*, eight companions are chosen to go with the hobbit Frodo on his mission to destroy the evil ring. The group includes elves, dwarves, and men to represent the different kinds of people who have resisted the evil Lord Sauron. The total number of the group is nine, to mirror the nine ring wraiths who follow Sauron. In our passage today, we'll see Jesus picking twelve Jewish men to be His official disciples, to mirror the twelve tribes of Israel in the Old Testament.

Read Mark 3:13–19

Where did Jesus go in verse 13?

+FUN FACT: After God rescued His people from slavery in Egypt, He met with their leader, Moses, on a mountaintop and gave him the law.

In verse 13, how does Mark describe the people Jesus called?

+FUN FACT: Throughout the Bible, we see God calling people, and He's still calling people today—including you, if you're trusting in Jesus! He doesn't call people because they're especially good, or smart, or attractive, or rich. He often calls the least impressive people because He wants them.

In verses 14–15, Jesus picks a smaller group of people out of the large group He has called. How many people does Jesus choose, and what are the three things He wants them to do?

In verse 16, who does Mark introduce us to first, and what's his nickname?

➜**FUN FACT:** Simon was the most common name for Jewish men in Jesus' day, so no wonder he needed a nickname! Simon's other name, Peter, means "rock." As we saw in the introduction, it seems that Mark's gospel is largely based on Simon Peter's memories!

Who are the next two people Mark introduces, and what nickname does Jesus give them?

➜**FUN FACT:** Along with Peter, these brothers—James and John—are in Jesus' inner circle, even within His small group of twelve. But we'll see as we read through Mark that even these three make big mistakes!

In verses 18–19, Mark gives us the rest of the names of Jesus' twelve disciples. What are their names? Write them below.

➥**FUN FACT:** According to an early tradition, Matthew wrote Matthew's gospel. His other name was Levi, and we met him on Day 6, when Jesus calls the tax collector Levi to follow Him.

Why do you think Mark gives us extra descriptions for James the son of Alpheus and Simon the Zealot?

_____

_____

_____

"Iscariot" probably refers to the place where Judas came from, but Mark gives us an extra description for him in verse 19. What does Mark say about Judas?

_____

_____

_____

How do you think it felt that one of Jesus' closest friends was the one who betrayed Him and, in the end, sent Him to His crucifixion?

_____

_____

_____

PRAY: Thank God that He has chosen *you* to be a follower of Jesus, with the special role of serving others with His love and telling others about Him. Ask Him to help you serve Him when things are hard and when following Jesus is unpopular.

JESUS' FAMILY THINKS HE'S CRAZY

In the Disney film *Moana*, Moana is chosen from early childhood for the mission of saving her people. The ocean gives her the magic stone that will enable their island to be restored. But her father doesn't understand that this is what she needs to do, and he keeps trying to stop her. He isn't Moana's enemy; he loves her. But he's opposing her. In our passage today, we'll see how Jesus' own family reacted to His mission, even while He was under attack, and how Jesus redefined what family means.

Read Mark 3:20–35

In verses 20–21, Jesus has gone back to His home base, and He's being swamped by crowds. How does His family react?

In verse 22, we hear that the "teachers of the law" have come from Jerusalem to check Jesus out. We met them in Mark 2:6–7, when Jesus told the paralyzed man that his sins were forgiven, and the teachers of the law thought Jesus was blaspheming because only God has the right to forgive sins. What do these teachers of the law say about Jesus in verse 22?

➔FUN FACT: Beelzebul was another name for Satan or the devil.

In verses 23–26, how does Jesus respond to the claim that He is possessed by Satan?

_____

_____

_____

In verse 27, Jesus draws an analogy. In this comparison, Satan is like the strong man. But Jesus is like an even stronger man who comes into the strong man's house and ties him up before taking things out of his house. Jesus has been casting out demons from people. So, in this analogy, what (or who) do you think Jesus has been plundering from Satan's house?

_____

_____

_____

In chapter 2, the teachers of the law thought Jesus was blaspheming against God by forgiving the paralyzed man's sins. In verses 28–29, who is really blaspheming against God?

_____

_____

_____

➔FUN FACT: In Mark 1:10, we saw the Holy Spirit descending on Jesus when He was baptized. In Matthew and Luke, we find that Jesus didn't have a human father, but that He was conceived by the Holy Spirit. So, Jesus is not possessed by Satan; He's filled with the Holy Spirit of God!

In verses 31–32, who arrives and what do they do?

_____

_____

_____

In verses 33–35, how does Jesus respond to the message from His family?

Jesus' reaction to His family seems shocking to us. What point do you think He is making by responding this way?

How does it make you feel to hear that other Christians are your family?

PRAY: If everyone in your family is a Christian and supports you in following Jesus, thank God for this and pray that He would encourage them in their faith. If some or all of your family members are not following Jesus, and maybe even oppose you in following Jesus, pray for the Lord to open their eyes to who Jesus is. Pray for strength to keep following Him despite opposition from your family.

JESUS TELLS A STORY
ABOUT GOD'S WORD

Our passage today is like a burger! Jesus tells a parable, and then He explains the meaning. The story and the explanation are like the top and bottom of the burger bun. But in the middle, He tells His disciples why He's using stories like this in His teaching. We're going to start with the top bun of the story. Then, we're going to chew on the meat in the middle, where Jesus explains why He's using parables. Finally, we're going to look at the bottom bun of the meaning.

Read Mark 4:1–20

In verse 1, where is Jesus and what is He doing?

Who is Jesus teaching?

In verses 3–8, Jesus tells a story about a farmer sowing seed. What four kinds of places did the seed fall?

What happened to the seed that fell on the path (v. 4)?

In verses 5–6, what happened to the seed that fell on rocky places and why?

In verse 7, what happened to the seed that fell among the thorns?

In verse 8, what happened to the seed that fell on good soil?

How does Jesus end His teaching (v. 9)?

In verses 10–11, Jesus is alone with His disciples, and they ask Him about the parables He was using to teach (we'll read more of them tomorrow). Jesus gave a strange answer. What does Jesus say has been given to His disciples in verse 11?

At the end of verse 12, what does Jesus say people might do if they really understood His message? What would happen in response?

✦FUN FACT: In verse 12, Jesus quotes from something the Lord says to the Old Testament prophet Isaiah (Isaiah 6:9–11). We might think that Jesus is telling stories to make it easy for people to understand, but He says the opposite. Only His true followers will get the meaning, not everyone in the crowd.

In verses 14–15, Jesus explains that the seed that landed on the path is people who hear God's Word, but Satan comes and takes it away—like a bird eating the seed—so they don't believe it. How can we be sure we are not like these people?

In verses 16–17, Jesus says the seed on the rocky ground is people who get excited when they first hear God's Word, but then stop following Jesus when things get hard. How can we avoid being like that?

In verses 18–19, Jesus says that the seed that lands among thorns is people who hear God's Word, but they want other things so much (for example, money or success) that these desires stop the seed from growing into a full plant. What things do you really want that might get in the way of you growing as a Christian?

In verse 20, Jesus says that the seed that lands on the good soil is people who hear God's Word and accept it. This seed will bear lots of fruit—like one little grain of wheat that grows to become a stalk with thirty, sixty, or a hundred grains! What do you think Jesus means by a Christian bearing fruit?

PRAY: Pray that Jesus would help you to hear His Word and receive it, so it will grow like the seed in the good soil!

JESUS TELLS THREE STORIES ABOUT GOD'S KINGDOM

In *The Lion, the Witch and the Wardrobe*, while the children are playing hide-and-seek in the professor's house, Lucy stumbles into the magical land of Narnia. It's like our world in some ways, and completely unlike it in others. When she gets out of Narnia again, Lucy tries to tell her brothers and sister about this other reality. But they don't believe her. In our passage today, Jesus tells a string of mini parables about the kingdom of God, which may seem just as unbelievable as the land of Narnia. Except that it's completely real.

Read Mark 4:21–34

The first thing Lucy sees in Narnia is a lamppost. The first thing Jesus talks about in this passage is a lamp. What question does Jesus ask in verse 21?

✦**FUN FACT:** In Jesus' day, people didn't have electric lights like we do. So, you couldn't just turn on a light. You had to light a lamp. You wouldn't do that just to put it under a cover!

In verse 22, Jesus explains that whatever is hidden is meant to be disclosed. How do you think God's kingdom might be like a lamp that reveals things that were previously hidden in the dark?

In verses 24–25, Jesus is talking about how we receive His Word. Today, He might have said, "You get out what you put in—with some extra!" The more we listen to Jesus, the more we hear. How does this help us understand what we read yesterday, when Jesus said that the secret of God had been given to His disciples, but that those who weren't truly following Him would hear but not understand (Mark 4:10–11)?

Jesus' offer of forgiveness for all who trust in Him is a free gift and not something we have to try to earn. It's really important that we don't get confused about that. He's done all the work for us! But Jesus teaches here that we do need to put effort into listening to God's Word. How can you grow in listening to Jesus in your own life?

In verses 26–29, Jesus tells another story about a man sowing seed. But the message is different from the parable of the sower that we looked at yesterday. After the sower in today's story has sowed the seed, how much work does he have to do to make it grow?

How do you think seeds growing roots underground and then sprouting up and becoming a great harvest is like the kingdom of God?

In verses 30–32, Jesus tells another parable connected to farming. What does He say about the mustard seed (v. 31)?

_____

_____

_____

What does Jesus say about the plant that the tiny mustard seed becomes (v. 32)?

_____

_____

_____

How do you think God's kingdom is like a tiny, unimpressive mustard seed that grows into a massive plant?

_____

_____

_____

You might be the only Christian in your group of friends at school or one of only a few Christians in your neighborhood, so to those around you it might seem like God's kingdom is very small and unimpressive. How can Jesus' parables that we've read today encourage us when it seems like hardly anyone around us is following Jesus?

_____

_____

_____

PRAY: Ask the Lord to help you grow as a listener to His Word, and ask Him to help you believe that His kingdom is growing all around you even when it doesn't look impressive. If you're feeling alone as a Christian at school or in your neighborhood, ask God for help to trust Him, and pray for each of your friends to come to know Him!

JESUS SHOWS HIS TERRIFYING POWER OVER NATURE

In the popular show *Avatar: The Last Airbender*, an avatar named Ang is born with the ability to control both wind and water. In our passage today, Jesus shows that He has that kind of control over nature in real life. We'll see His disciples getting really scared in the middle of a massive storm—and even more scared after Jesus uses His amazing superpowers to calm the storm!

Read Mark 4:35–41

Jesus was sitting in a boat at the edge of a lake when He taught the crowd with parables. In verses 35–36, what time of day is it, and what do Jesus and His disciples do?

What happened in verse 37? (A "furious squall" means a massive storm.)

What is Jesus doing in verse 36?

✦FUN FACT: Some of Jesus' disciples are fishermen (see Mark 1:16–20), so you might think they'd know what do to in a storm. But it seems like this storm is terrifying even for them!

How do Jesus' disciples react in verse 38?

_____

_____

_____

Why do you think the disciples thought that Jesus didn't care?

_____

_____

_____

✦FUN FACT: The word "rebuke" means to tell off sharply or correct. Later in Mark's gospel, we'll see Jesus rebuking His disciples at various points when they completely misunderstand Him.

What did Jesus do in verse 39?

_____

_____

_____

What would happen if you, or your parent, or your school principal, or the president of the United States rebuked the wind?

_____

_____

_____

In verse 39, what happened when Jesus rebuked the wind and told the waves to be quiet and still?

_____

_____

_____

What did Jesus ask the disciples in verse 40?

_____

_____

_____

You might think that the disciples would stop being afraid now that the storm was over. But how do they feel according to verse 41?

_____

_____

_____

⇒✦FUN FACT: As we walk through Mark's gospel, we'll often see people being terrified when they witness Jesus' power. Try to spot those moments as we go along. They'll help you understand what happens at the end of Mark!

What question do the disciples ask?

_____

_____

_____

What is the answer to their question in verse 41?

_____

_____

_____

⇒✦FUN FACT: When Jesus tells the paralyzed man his sins are forgiven, the teachers of the law think to themselves, "Why does this fellow talk like that? He's blaspheming! Who can forgive sins but God alone?" The answer to, "Who can forgive sins?" is the same as the answer to the disciples' question in Mark 4:41: God alone.

 PRAY: Praise Jesus for His power, even over the wind and the waves! Ask Him to help you see how amazing He is and to trust Him when your life feels like a massive storm raging all around you.

JESUS SHOWS HIS TERRIFYING POWER OVER DEMONS

In *Harry Potter and the Chamber of Secrets*, the evil Lord Voldemort has possessed the little sister of Harry's best friend, Ron. Voldemort is controlling Ginny and making her do terrible things she would never have done by herself. But at the end of the story, Harry confronts Voldemort and attacks the diary that Voldemort has been using to possess Ginny. Voldemort's power gets sucked out of Ginny and she's back to normal. In our passage today, Jesus calls evil spirits out of a man who has been completely overrun by them, and once again, we'll see how terrifying Jesus' power is.

Read Mark 5:1–20

How does Mark describe the demon-possessed man in verses 3–5?

In verse 6, what does the man do when he sees Jesus?

In verse 7, what does the man say to Jesus?

How is this similar to what the first demon-possessed man said to Jesus (see Mark 1:24)?

_____

_____

_____

In verse 9, what does the man say when Jesus asks his name?

_____

_____

➤FUN FACT: In the Roman army, a "legion" was a group of about 5,500 soldiers who worked together. So, the name Legion suggests that the man has been possessed by many demons and that they're like a strong fighting force.

In verse 12, what do the demons ask Jesus to do?

_____

_____

_____

How does Jesus respond to the request (v. 13)?

_____

_____

_____

What happens when the demons go into the pigs (v. 13)?

_____

_____

_____

How does this show the power of the demons and the even greater power of Jesus?

_____

_____

_____

In verses 14–15, the pig herders run to tell everyone they know what has happened and people come to see for themselves. What do the people find when they come, and how do they react?

_____

_____

_____

Why do you think the people are afraid?

_____

_____

_____

In verse 17, the people beg Jesus to leave their region. But in verse 18, the man who used to be demon-possessed begs Jesus for something else. What is his request?

_____

_____

_____

In verse 19, what does Jesus tell the man to do instead?

_____

_____

_____

Jesus tells the man to tell his people how much the Lord (God) has done for him. But what does the man tell people in verse 20?

_____

_____

_____

How does this story help us see that Jesus is God?

_____

_____

_____

PRAY: Praise Jesus for His power over the spiritual forces of evil, and ask Him to help you be like the man who was set free from demons and told everyone he knew how much Jesus had done for him.

JESUS HEALS
TWO DAUGHTERS

Right before Jesus heals the paralyzed man, He says, "Son, your sins are forgiven!" Today, we see Jesus healing two daughters, one of whom is about your age. We'll see today that you're never too young, too unclean, or too dead to be restored by Jesus!

Read Mark 5:21–43

In verse 22, who falls at Jesus' feet and what does he beg Jesus to do?

_____

_____

⇒**FUN FACT:**
According to Jewish law, this woman would have been officially "unclean" because of her bleeding. When women were having their period, they were unable to go into the temple to worship, and this woman had been bleeding for twelve years straight. If someone touched her, they'd be "unclean" as well and would have to wash themselves in a special way to get clean again. So, lots of people would have been avoiding this woman for years.

While Jesus is on His way to Jairus's house, Mark introduces us to one woman in the crowd. What do we learn about this woman (vv. 25–26)?

_____

_____

In verses 27–28, what does the woman do and why?

_____

_____

In verse 29, what happens to the woman?

In verses 30–31, Jesus realized that power has gone out from Him, so He asks, "Who touched my clothes?" Why do the disciples think this is an odd question?

In verse 33, how does the woman react when she realized Jesus is going to keep looking until He finds her? Why do you think she was so scared?

How does Jesus react to her in verse 34, and how is this different from what she might have expected?

✦FUN FACT: This is the only time in Mark's gospel that Jesus calls someone "daughter." He doesn't just heal this woman; He includes her in His family.

What bad news arrives in verse 35?

_____

_____

In verse 36, what does Jesus say to Jairus?

_____

_____

In verse 38, when Jesus gets to Jairus's house, what's everyone doing?

_____

_____

In verses 39–40, what does Jesus say and how do the people react?

_____

_____

✦FUN FACT: As we saw in the introduction, the New Testament is written in Greek. But Jews of Jesus' day mostly speak a language called Aramaic. A few times in the Gospels, we get to hear the Aramaic words that Jesus uses.

In verse 41, what does Jesus do and what does He say?

_____

_____

_____

In verse 42, what does the dead girl do?

_____

_____

_____

In verse 42, we find out the girl had been alive for the same number of years that the woman had been bleeding (v. 25). How do these two stories together help us see Jesus' love and power?

_____

_____

_____

PRAY: Thank Jesus for His tender, individual love for each of us, no matter how old we are, how sick we are, or how much other people might not want to be near us. Pray that He would help you feel that love, especially when you're feeling desperate, like the bleeding woman.

Well done for working through to the end of Act 2! You're making great progress through Mark's awesome gospel!

JESUS GROWS

HIS KINGDOM

FAMILY

Act 2 began with Jesus being rejected by the religious and political leaders but calling His apostles. And now, Act 3 begins with Jesus being rejected in His own hometown but sending His apostles out with power to preach and heal. In this act, we see Jesus growing His kingdom family.

In the Old Testament book of Exodus, God led His people out of Egypt, brought them through the Red Sea on dry land, fed them with bread in the wilderness, and gave them His law. In Act 3, we see Jesus miraculously feeding five thousand Jewish families, who had come to hear Him preach and see Him heal. He walks on water as if it were dry land, and He teaches God's law. It's like Jesus is an even better Moses!

In this act, we will also see Jesus breaking down the barrier between the Jews and non-Jews (known as Gentiles) by showing we're all sinners before God, letting a Gentile woman join the family and share the bread, healing a deaf man in a Gentile region, and feeding four thousand families in a Gentile area. Jesus is opening God's kingdom up not only to Jews, but to Gentiles as well! But His disciples still don't understand. Finally, Jesus heals a blind man in two stages—not because He's incompetent, but so that this healing can be a picture of the gradual opening up of His disciples' eyes.

Act 1: Mark 1–2
—
JESUS IS
GOD'S PROMISED
KING

Act 2: Mark 3–5
—
JESUS STARTS
HIS KINGDOM
FAMILY

Act 3: Mark 6–8:26
—
JESUS GROWS
HIS KINGDOM
FAMILY

JESUS IS REJECTED IN HIS HOMETOWN AND SENDS THE APOSTLES

Jesus didn't come from an impressive place. He came from a small town—more a village, really—called Nazareth, in the northern region of Galilee. It was many miles from Jerusalem, which was the center of Jewish life and worship. When one of Jesus' disciples told his friend Nathanael that he thought he'd found God's promised king and said that it was "Jesus of Nazareth," Nathanael replied, "Nazareth! Can anything good come from there?" (John 1:46). Today, we're going to read about Jesus going back to His hometown and how the people there reacted to Him.

Read Mark 6:1–13

In verse 2, where is Jesus, what day is it, and what is He doing?

In verse 2, how did the people of Jesus' hometown seem to react at first?

What question do they ask at the beginning of verse 3?

→FUN FACT: In Jesus' day, most boys would have been trained to do the same job as their father. Jesus' adoptive father, Joseph, was a carpenter (Matthew 13:55), so Jesus had worked as a carpenter too before He started His public ministry.

What other questions do people ask in verse 3?

_____

_____

_____

How do they react at the end of verse 3?

_____

_____

_____

How does Jesus explain their response (v. 4)?

_____

_____

_____

→FUN FACT: A prophet in the Old Testament was someone who spoke God's words to people about the past, present, and future.

From what you've seen of Jesus so far in Mark's gospel, why do you think Jesus refers to Himself as a prophet in verse 4?

_____

_____

_____

In verse 5, Mark says that Jesus could not do any miracles in Nazareth, except for a few healing miracles, and that Jesus was amazed at their lack of faith. We've seen already in Mark's gospel that Jesus has power to do whatever He wants, so what was stopping Him from doing more miracles in Nazareth?

In verses 6–7, Jesus continues teaching from village to village and sends His twelve disciples out in pairs. What authority does He give them (v. 7)?

What instructions does Jesus give His disciples in verses 8–11?

How would you feel if you were going on a long journey by foot and you weren't allowed to take a change of clothes or any food or money? How do you think this might have helped the disciples to trust God?

What two potential reactions to the disciples' arrival do we see in verses 10–11?

_____

_____

_____

⇒✦**FUN FACT:** When Jewish rabbis came home after traveling to foreign lands, they would shake the dust off their clothes.

According to verse 12, what message did the apostles preach when they went from town to town?

_____

_____

_____

Why do you think Jesus' call for people to repent—which means to say you're sorry to God for your sins and to turn from them—is hard for people to accept today?

_____

_____

_____

PRAY: If you have not yet repented and turned to Jesus, ask God to help you do that now. If you have, ask Jesus to help you when you feel rejected by people around you because of your faith.

JOHN THE BAPTIST'S TRAGIC END

When Jesus was a toddler, King Herod the Great tried to get Him killed (see Matthew 2:16). But Jesus escaped and King Herod himself died not long afterward. Two of his sons went on to be rulers of different regions, and in our passage today, we meet one of them—Herod Antipas— who was ruling over Galilee during Jesus' lifetime. In the story, Herod Antipas ends up being like his father: a killer of the innocent.

Read Mark 6:14–29

In verse 14, who heard about the ministry of Jesus and His disciples?

➡ **FUN FACT:** John the Baptist was a relative of Jesus, and as we saw in Mark 1:1–8, he was sent by God to be a prophet, preparing the way for Jesus' ministry. John dressed and acted like Elijah, one of the great Old Testament prophets. Instead of dying, Elijah had been taken up into heaven (2 Kings 2:11), and many Jews believed that Elijah would come back before the final judgment day.

According to verses 14–15, who were different groups of people saying Jesus was?

In verse 16, what did Herod Antipas say when he heard about Jesus?

In verses 17–28, we hear how Herod came to have John the Baptist beheaded. According to verses 17–18, what did Herod do first and why?

In verses 19–20, why couldn't Herodias get John killed like she wanted?

In verse 21, Herod threw a massive birthday party for himself, and Herodias's daughter danced for Herod and his guests. What did Herod offer her (v. 23)?

In verse 24, Herodias's daughter asks her mother what she should request. What does her mother say she should ask for?

In verse 26, how did Herod feel when he heard her request for John the Baptist's head on a plate?

In verse 27, what does Herod do?

_____

_____

_____

In verse 28, what does Herodias's daughter do when she gets John the Baptist's head on a plate?

_____

_____

How does this story make sense of Herod's response to Jesus in verse 16?

_____

_____

_____

How would this story have been different if Herod had repented when John the Baptist called him out on his sin?

_____

_____

_____

How would this story have been different if Herod had said no to Herodias's daughter's request, instead of being too embarrassed in front of his guests to do the right thing?

_____

_____

_____

PRAY: Ask God for courage to tell the truth like John the Baptist, even when you know it will get you into trouble, and not to give into peer pressure to do the wrong thing, like Herod. Thank God that Jesus came to be the real hero and to take all our sins away, including the times we fail to stand up for the truth in front of our friends.

JESUS FEEDS FIVE THOUSAND JEWISH FAMILIES

Think of a time when you have felt hungry. Really hungry. Now, imagine you had been in the middle of a wilderness at that time and not near any house or store or restaurant where you could get food. Think about how you would feel. Today, we're going to read about a time when lots and lots of people were hungry and Jesus gave them so much food they couldn't even eat it all!

Read Mark 6:30–44

In verses 31–32, how does Jesus show His care for His disciples?

_____

_____

_____

What happened when Jesus and His disciples tried to go to a quiet place to get some rest (v. 33)?

_____

_____

_____

How do we see Jesus' care for the crowds who come to Him (v. 34)?

_____

_____

➔**FUN FACT:** In the Old Testament, God is often described as a shepherd to His people. For example, Psalm 23 begins, "The Lord is my shepherd, I lack nothing" (Psalm 23:1).

What do the disciples tell Jesus to do in verse 36?

_____

_____

_____

How does Jesus respond in verse 37?

_____

_____

_____

What problem do the disciples raise in verse 37?

_____

_____

_____

In verse 38, Jesus asks them to see how much bread they have. How much food do they come back with for the massive crowd?

_____

_____

_____

What do you think you would have said if you had been in Jesus' position, and it turned out there were only five loaves of bread and two fish to feed a whole crowd of people?

_____

_____

_____

In verse 41, what does Jesus do with the five loaves of bread and the two fish?

In verse 42, what happens, and why is it surprising?

➡**FUN FACT:** In the Old Testament book of Exodus, God's people wander in the wilderness, and they run out of bread. So, God makes stuff appear all over the ground every day. The people call it "manna," which means "What is it?" But it turns out that you could make this manna into bread, and they live on manna bread for forty years!

In verse 43, how much food was left over after all the people had eaten? Do you think that was more or less than the amount of food that Jesus started with?

In verse 44, how many men had eaten?

✦**FUN FACT:** Men would have been counted as representatives of their families, so Jesus actually feeds far more people, because there would be lots of women and children too!

How does this miracle remind us of when God made manna in the wilderness?

How does this story help us to trust God to take care of us today?

_____

_____

_____

PRAY: Tell your heavenly Father about something that you're worried about, and ask Him to help you in that situation. Ask Him as well to help you trust Him when it seems like everything is going wrong.

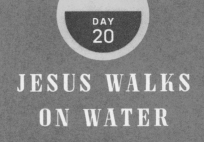

JESUS WALKS ON WATER

In Disney's *Frozen 2*, Princess Elsa discovers that as well as having ice powers, she's able to ride on water. She finds this out the hard way! First, she's attacked by a creature that looks like a horse made of water. Then, she learns to ride the horse. In Mark 4:35–41, we saw how Jesus calmed a massive storm at sea just with His words. Today, we're going to see Jesus walking on water.

Read Mark 6:45–56

What two groups of people did Jesus send away in verse 45?

_____

_____

_____

In verse 46, Jesus is alone. What does He do and where?

_____

_____

_____

✦FUN FACT: In the book of Exodus, God makes a path of dry land through the middle of the Red Sea, and Moses leads God's people through the sea.

In verse 47, where was the boat that Jesus' disciples were in, and where was Jesus?

_____

_____

_____

In verse 48, why were the disciples finding it hard to row the boat?

What did Jesus do right before dawn?

In verses 49–50, what did the disciples think and how did they feel?

➡*FUN FACT:* In Matthew's gospel, we find out that Peter said, "Lord, if it's you, tell me to come to you on the water." Jesus replied, "Come." So, Peter got out of the boat and started walking toward Jesus. But when Peter saw the wind, he got scared and started to sink. He cried out, "Lord, save me!" and Jesus reached out His hand and caught him. "You of little faith," said Jesus, "Why did you doubt?" (Matthew 14:28–31).

How do you think you would feel if you saw someone walking on the rough waves of the sea in the night?

In verse 50, what did Jesus say to His disciples when He saw they were afraid?

In verse 51, what did Jesus do and what happened when He did it?

At the end of verse 51, how did the disciples react?

How does Mark explain their reaction in verse 52?

What do you think they should have realized about Jesus when He provided food for thousands of people from five loaves and two fish? In verse 54, what happened when Jesus and His disciples got out of the boat at Gennesaret?

In verse 55, what did people do?

In verse 56, what happened to sick people who even touched the hem of Jesus' cloak?

_____

_____

_____

What do the three stories of Jesus feeding thousands of people, walking on water, and healing people who just touched His clothes tell us about Jesus?

_____

_____

_____

PRAY: Ask Jesus to help you believe that He really is the Son of God with power over food, seas, sickness, life, and death.

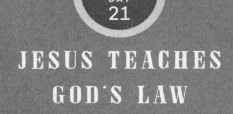

JESUS TEACHES
GOD'S LAW

Ever since Miranda was a little kid, she's always spotted the exception to any rule. If she was told, "You must never jump out of the window," she would reply, "Unless the house is on fire, and then you *should* jump out." She was right. Rules are put in place for our good, but sometimes there's a good reason to break a rule. In our passage today, we'll see the Pharisees criticizing Jesus' disciples for breaking the rules, which weren't even really part of God's law in the first place. But Jesus shows that the Pharisees are the ones who are actually failing to follow God's law.

Read Mark 7:1–13

In verse 1, where had the Pharisees and teachers of the law come from to check Jesus out?

In verse 2, what did they notice about some of Jesus' disciples?

In verses 3–4, what extra information does Mark give us about the Pharisees to help us understand?

What do the Pharisees ask Jesus in verse 5?

_____

_____

_____

What does Jesus call the Pharisees in verse 6?

_____

_____

➡️*FUN FACT:* The Pharisees follow lots of extra rules that have been added over time to the laws that God gave to His people. For example, if God's law said to wash your hands before eating, the "tradition of the elders," which the Pharisees follow, might add extra rules about *how* you have to wash your hands. They aren't trying to avoid spreading germs; they are trying to make themselves "clean" before God.

➡️*FUN FACT:* A hypocrite is someone who tells other people to do something they're not doing themselves. In our family, for example, Rebecca and Bryan are hypocrites when they scold Miranda and Eliza for their messy bedroom, because Rebecca and Bryan's bedroom is a mess as well!

In verse 6, Jesus quotes from the Old Testament prophet Isaiah and says Isaiah was talking about the Pharisees. What does Jesus say about their lips, and what does He say about their hearts?

_____

_____

_____

What does verse 7 say about how the Pharisees worship God?

_____

_____

_____

➡️*FUN FACT:* "In vain" means failing to do something you're trying to do. For example, if you were playing soccer and you missed your shot, you could say, "I tried in vain to score a goal!"

In verse 8, what does Jesus say they're letting go of and what does He say they're holding on to?

_____

_____

_____

In verse 10, Jesus gives an example of a law God gave to Moses. What was the law and what was the punishment if you did the opposite?

_____

_____

_____

When people grew old in Jesus' day, they didn't get money for retirement. Their children were meant to look after them. But in verse 11, Jesus says the Pharisees are encouraging people to do something else with their money: dedicate it to the temple in worship of God instead of giving the money to their parents. How is this really breaking God's law even though it looks like a religious thing to do?

_____

_____

_____

How are we sometimes like the Pharisees: talking a lot about following God and singing worship songs at church, but not actually loving Him with our hearts and loving others as He tells us to?

_____

_____

_____

PRAY: Ask Jesus to help you not to be a hypocrite but to love God in your heart and show your love to God by loving others.

JESUS SHOWS BOTH JEWS AND GENTILES ARE UNCLEAN

Have you ever read a comic book? If you have, you'll know that sometimes a bubble like a little cloud over someone's head shows you what they're thinking. Imagine you had a bubble over your head all the time, where people could read what you were thinking. Wouldn't that be terrible? They'd see not just your nice thoughts but also your mean or shameful ones. In our passage today, Jesus explains that it's not the food that goes into our bodies that makes us unclean, but the thoughts and actions that come out of our hearts.

Read Mark 7:14–23

What does Jesus say to the crowd in verse 15?

_____

_____

_____

We saw yesterday that the Pharisees were complaining that Jesus' disciples were defiling themselves by eating without first washing their hands in the right way. But in verses 18–19, Jesus explains why the things we eat can't make us unclean before God. What does Jesus say in verse 19 about where food goes and where it doesn't go?

_____

_____

_____

What comment does Mark make at the end of verse 19?

⇢FUN FACT: Under the Old Testament law, some kinds of food are seen as unclean. For example, God's people are not allowed to eat pigs or camels because they are in the category of unclean animals (see Leviticus 11:1–8). This was one of the ways in which God's people are set apart from other peoples.

Why do you think Jesus had the right to say that all foods were now okay for God's people to eat?

How do you think Jesus' Jewish hearers might have felt about Jesus breaking down this big dividing wall between Jews and Gentiles?

In verse 20, what does Jesus say does make us unclean?

According to verse 21, where do our evil thoughts come from?

In verse 21, Jesus lists a lot of different kinds of sin. Write the example of sin that Jesus gives in the boxes on the left. Look at the definitions on the right if there are some words you don't know.

Sexual immorality	Any kind of sexual behavior outside of marriage
Theft	Stealing
Murder	Killing someone
Adultery	Cheating on your husband or wife with someone else
Greed	Taking more than you need
Malice	Nastiness
Deceit	Lying
Lewdness	Inappropriate behavior
Envy	Resenting what other people have
Slander	Saying nasty things about someone
Arrogance	Being full of pride
Folly	Not being stupid, but arrogantly rejecting God

If someone could see the thought bubble over your head between now and this time tomorrow, which of the sins Jesus lists do you think they'd notice?

_____

_____

_____

_____

How does verse 23 help us to see that even the sins that don't seem as bad to us make us unclean before God?

_____

_____

_____

_____

⇒**FUN FACT:** People sometimes claim that Jesus never teaches about same-sex sexual relationships. But the word translated "sexual immorality" means any sexual relationship outside of marriage. In the Roman Empire, just like in our culture today, lots of sexual relationships outside of marriage were seen as okay, including same-sex sexual relationships. But Jesus makes it clear here that sex only belongs in marriage, and we'll see in chapter 10 that Jesus defines marriage as one man and one woman made "one flesh" for life.

PRAY: Ask Jesus to help you see the sinful things that come out of your heart and say you're sorry for them. Thank Jesus that when He died on the cross, He took all our sins away so we can be completely forgiven and clean before God. Praise Jesus that He knows all the thoughts in your thought bubble and that He still loves you more than you can possibly imagine!

JESUS LETS A GENTILE WOMAN JOIN THE FAMILY

Yesterday, we saw Jesus debating with some of the Jewish leaders. He called them hypocrites and went on to break down a major Jew/Gentile divide by saying that all foods were clean and that uncleanness comes from our hearts, not from what we eat. Today, we'll see Jesus going to a Gentile region and having a different kind of debate with a Gentile woman, which shows that Gentiles can join God's family as well.

Read Mark 7:24–30

In verse 24, where did Jesus go to?

⟞**✦FUN FACT:** Tyre and Sidon were in a region named Phoenicia. It was a Gentile area where not many Jews would have lived, and Tyre and Sidon were known for idolatry and sin. So, it's interesting that Jesus goes there after fighting with the Jewish leaders!

In verse 24, what did Jesus do when He got to this area, and what did He want?

In verse 25, a woman heard that Jesus was in town and came to Him. What was her problem?

What did the woman do in verse 25?

_____

_____

_____

How does Mark describe this woman in verse 26?

_____

_____

_____

≡✦FUN FACT: Mark's description of the woman emphasizes her non-Jewishness.

What does the woman beg Jesus to do in verse 26?

_____

_____

_____

How does Jesus respond in verse 27?

_____

_____

_____

≡✦FUN FACT: Jesus' words sound shocking to us. But His Jewish disciples would have nodded along. In the Old Testament, God often referred to the Israelites as His children, and Jewish people of Jesus' day would sometimes have called Gentiles "dogs."

How might we expect the woman to feel when Jesus uses the word "dog" to describe her as a Gentile?

_____

_____

_____

We might have replied, "How dare you call me a dog!" But how does the woman respond (v. 28)?

What does Jesus say when this woman shows her humble faith in Him (v. 29)?

FUN FACT: When Matthew tells this same story, he includes Jesus saying, "Woman, you have great faith!" because Jesus is so impressed with her.

How does yesterday's passage in which Jesus broke down a big Jew/ Gentile divide help us understand today's passage?

Where in Mark's gospel have we seen Jewish people (the children) eating all they want from Jesus?

What can we learn from this Gentile woman about the need to give up all our pride when we come to Jesus?

What can we learn from this Gentile woman about bringing our greatest need to Jesus?

_____

_____

_____

PRAY: Ask God to give you humble faith in Jesus, like the Gentile woman in this story.

JESUS HEALS A DEAF MAN
IN A GENTILE AREA

Jesus' visit to Tyre and Sidon and His healing of the Gentile woman's daughter was the beginning of a string of miracles that Jesus did for Gentiles who had faith in Him. We'll read about another one today. Jesus healed the Gentile woman's daughter from a distance: He just says she's healed, and she is. But in our story today, Jesus takes multiple steps to heal a man who is brought to Him.

Read Mark 7:31–37

What region did Jesus go to when He left Tyre and Sidon (v. 31)?

_____

_____

_____

✦FUN FACT: Decapolis was a Gentile region with ten cities. The Greek word for ten is *deca*, and the word for city is *polis*, so that's how Decapolis got its name. This is also the region where the man whom Jesus heals from a legion of demons came from and where he returns to and tells everyone there how much Jesus has done for him (Mark 5:20).

In verse 32, some people bring a man to Jesus. What two problems does the man have?

_____

_____

_____

What do the people ask Jesus to do (v. 32)?

If Jesus was just wanting to show off His power, He would have healed the man in front of the crowd. What does Jesus do instead (v. 33)?

What did Jesus do to the man's ears (v. 33)?

What did Jesus do to the man's tongue (v. 33)?

Why do you think Jesus looked up to heaven before speaking in verse 34?

Do you think Jesus had to pray before He could heal someone? If not, why not?

What did Jesus say after He looked up to heaven and sighed, and what did it mean?

FUN FACT: This is the second time in Mark's gospel that we get to hear some Aramaic, which would have been Jesus' first language. The first time was when He raised the dead twelve-year-old girl back to life and said, "Talitha koum," which means, "Little girl, I say to you get up!" (Mark 5:41).

What happened to the man in verse 35?

What instruction did Jesus give to the people who had seen Him heal the man in verse 36?

Did the people follow Jesus' instruction?

What were they saying about Jesus (v. 37)?

PRAY: Thank God that Jesus cares for you, just like He cared about the man He healed. Praise Him for His power and His love for all kinds of people: Jewish and Gentile, healthy and sick.

JESUS FEEDS FOUR THOUSAND FAMILIES IN A GENTILE AREA

Remember how Jesus told the Gentile woman that it wasn't right to take the children's bread and throw it to the dogs? Today, we see Jesus doing a miracle just like His miracle of feeding five thousand Jewish families; except this time, He does it for Gentiles too! But His disciples still don't understand.

Read Mark 8:1–21

What problem did the people have in verse 1?

How does Jesus say He feels about this crowd of hungry people?

➥✦FUN FACT: Having compassion on someone means feeling sorry for them or caring for them. We frequently see Jesus in the Gospels showing compassion.

Why is the question the disciples ask in verse 4 a silly question?

How much food do the disciples have this time (v. 5 and v. 7)?

What does Jesus do with the loaves and the fish (vv. 6–7)?

What did the people do (v. 8)?

How many baskets of broken pieces of food did the disciples pick up (v. 8)?

How many people had eaten (v. 9)?

How does this miracle show that Jesus has enough spiritual bread for everyone—including the Gentiles?

Who came to Jesus in verse 11 and why?

_____

_____

_____

What did the Pharisees ask Jesus for, and how does He respond?

_____

What did Jesus tell His disciples to watch out for in verse 15?

_____

_____

_____

How did the disciples misunderstand what Jesus meant (v. 16)?

_____

_____

⇛*FUN FACT:* When God rescued His people from Egypt, He tells them to bake bread without yeast (or leaven) and eat it at the special meal. So, every year, the Jews celebrate the Passover and eat bread with no yeast for a week. The Pharisees are in many ways the opposite of the followers of Herod, who is the ruler set up by the Romans. But they have one thing in common: they want Jesus dead (Mark 3:6).

What does Jesus ask the disciples in verse 17?

_____

_____

_____

What body parts does Jesus say must not be working for His disciples (v. 18)?

_____

_____

_____

In verses 19–20, what miracles does Jesus remind His disciples about?

_____

_____

_____

Why was it silly of the disciples to think that Jesus was complaining that they'd forgotten to bring bread?

_____

_____

_____

PRAY: Thank Jesus that He has more than enough for everyone who puts their trust in Him. Ask Jesus to help you really see who He is, unlike His disciples in today's passage. Pray for a friend who doesn't trust in Jesus yet to start seeing who He is.

JESUS HEALS A BLIND MAN IN TWO STAGES

In the Disney film *Tangled*, Rapunzel's tears save Eugene's life by healing the stab wound the horrible witch Gothel has inflicted on him. But in the original fairy tale, the prince falls from Rapunzel's tower and is blinded by a thorn bush until Rapunzel's tears drop in his eyes and heal them. Today, we'll see Jesus heal a blind man, not with tears, but with His spit!

Read Mark 8:22–26

Where did Jesus and His disciples go in verse 22?

_____

_____

_____

➤*FUN FACT:* Three of Jesus' disciples—Peter, Andrew, and Philip—came from Bethsaida (see John 1:44; 12:21).

What happened when Jesus arrived in Bethsaida (v. 22)?

_____

_____

_____

Where did Jesus take the blind man (v. 23)?

_____

_____

_____

What two things did Jesus do to the blind man (v. 23)?

_____

_____

What question did Jesus ask the man (v. 23)?

_____

_____

Usually, Jesus heals people in one go. But what does verse 24 tell us about the man's eyesight after Jesus spat on his eyes and put His hands on him?

_____

_____

_____

In our passage yesterday, Jesus asked His disciples, "Do you have eyes but fail to see?" How is the blind man in this moment a bit like Jesus' disciples?

_____

_____

_____

What did Jesus do next (v. 25)?

_____

_____

What happened to the man (v. 25)?

_____

_____

➡✦FUN FACT: Mark tells us three times that the man could see again: "His eyes were opened, his sight was restored, and he saw everything clearly." This guy could really, really, really see!

Who did the work to get the man from being able to see only a little to being able to see everything clearly?

➡✦FUN FACT: We know that Jesus can heal people just with His words, even if they aren't there, like He did with the Gentile woman's daughter. But here, Jesus goes through multiple steps to heal the blind man—just like when Jesus healed the deaf man who could not speak properly by putting his fingers in his ears and putting spit on his mouth and saying, "Be opened."

How does this two-stage miracle help us understand Jesus' work in the lives of the disciples?

How does this miracle help us understand Jesus' work in our own lives?

PRAY: If you believe that Jesus is the Son of God, who came to die for your sins and be raised from the dead so you can live with Him forever, thank God for opening your eyes to see who Jesus is! If you're not sure what you think of Jesus yet, ask God to open your eyes just like Jesus opened the eyes of the blind man.

You've made it to the end of Act 3, so you're at the halfway mark of Mark! Well done!

JESUS TURNS

GOD'S KINGDOM

UPSIDE DOWN

Act 4 starts well. Peter declares that Jesus is God's promised King! But then Jesus teaches that He's going to be rejected and killed before rising again, and Peter thinks He must have got it wrong. Peter doesn't understand that Jesus has to die. But Jesus makes it clear that He does: His kingdom is all upside down because the King has come to serve.

Then something wonderful happens: Jesus takes three of His disciples—Peter, James, and John—up on a mountaintop. There, they get a glimpse of His glory and hear God's voice saying, "This is my Son whom I love. Listen to him!" But they still don't get it. When Jesus predicts His death again, His disciples start arguing about which of them is the greatest. Jesus has to explain that in His kingdom, whoever wants to be first must be last.

Continuing to challenge expectations about status, Jesus defends women, welcomes children, and teaches that it's harder for a rich man to get into God's kingdom than for a camel to go through the eye of a needle! Then, He teaches His disciples once again that He's going to die. This time, James and John are the ones who mess up. Jesus has to explain again that His kingdom works upside down. Why? Because even He did not come to be served, but to serve, and to give His life as a ransom for many.

Act 3 ended with a blind man being healed, and Act 4 ends that same way.

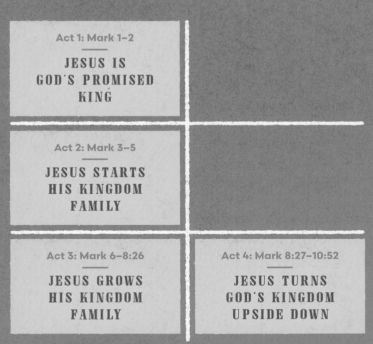

Act 1: Mark 1–2

JESUS IS GOD'S PROMISED KING

Act 2: Mark 3–5

JESUS STARTS HIS KINGDOM FAMILY

Act 3: Mark 6–8:26

JESUS GROWS HIS KINGDOM FAMILY

Act 4: Mark 8:27–10:52

JESUS TURNS GOD'S KINGDOM UPSIDE DOWN

PETER GETS THAT JESUS IS GOD'S PROMISED KING

In J. R. R. Tolkien's *The Fellowship of the Ring*, representatives of elves, dwarves, and men gather for a council to decide what to do with the ring. The man Boromir asks skeptically who Aragorn is, looking at his weather-stained cloak. The half-elven ruler Elrond, who has gathered the council, explains that Aragorn is the true heir to the throne of Gondor. Aragorn is the king everyone's been waiting for. But not everyone recognizes him. Today, we'll see that Jesus is God's long-promised King. But He's very different from what people expected.

Read Mark 8:27–30

What did Jesus ask His disciples while they were traveling around (v. 27)?

_____

_____

_____

What is the first answer Jesus' disciples give (v. 28)?

_____

_____

_____

What had happened to John the Baptist? (If you don't remember, look back at Mark 6:14–29.)

_____

_____

_____

According to Mark 6:14–16, some people thought that Jesus was John the Baptist raised from the dead. But other people had a different idea. What was the second answer Jesus' disciples gave to His question (v. 28)?

_____

_____

_____

✦FUN FACT: Elijah was a great Old Testament prophet who was taken up into heaven in a chariot of fire (2 Kings 2:11)! At the very end of the Old Testament, God spoke through the prophet Malachi telling His people to remember the law He gave through Moses on Mount Horeb and promising that He would send the prophet Elijah to them again before the "great and dreadful day of the LORD" (Malachi 4:4–5).

What was the third answer the disciples gave to Jesus' question (v. 28)?

_____

_____

What does Jesus ask the disciples in verse 29?

_____

_____

How does Peter answer (v. 29)?

_____

_____

✦FUN FACT: As we learned on Day 1, the words "Messiah" and "Christ" mean "God's anointed King." At the time when Jesus walked this earth, many Jews were longing for God to send the King He'd promised through His prophets. The people were hoping that God's King would kick the Romans out and make the Jewish people into a powerful nation once again.

How does Jesus respond when Peter says Jesus is the Messiah (v. 30)?

This is not the first time Jesus has told people to keep quiet about Him. Read Mark 1:34. Who does Jesus order to keep quiet about who He is here?

Read Mark 1:43–44. Who does Jesus order to keep quiet here?

Read Mark 7:36. Who does Jesus order to keep quiet here?

Can you think of a time when you've told someone to keep a secret, not because you didn't want anyone else to know ever, but because it wasn't time for them to know yet? Jesus is God's promised King. But it wasn't time for that to be proclaimed just yet. As we'll see tomorrow, even Jesus' disciples didn't understand what kind of King He was.

 PRAY: Imagine what it would be like to meet the greatest king in history or from your favorite story—like Aragorn in the Lord of the Rings. Then thank God that you get to meet an even greater King—King Jesus—and that He loves you so much He was ready to die for you!

JESUS SAYS HE'S GOING TO DIE AND RISE AGAIN

In Tolkien's *The Return of the King*, Aragorn has to go through the Paths of the Dead if he's going to be able to defeat his enemies in the coming battle. A brave woman named Éowyn tries to talk him out of it. She thinks he's just walking into death with no hope of coming out on the other side. But Aragorn knows what he must do. Today, we'll see Jesus explaining that while He is God's promised King, He's come to die. But He will also walk through death and come out victorious on the other side.

Read Mark 8:31–33

What name does Jesus use for Himself in verse 31?

What terrible things does Jesus tell His disciples must happen to the amazing Son of Man in verse 31?

➡ **FUN FACT:** Jesus has already called Himself "the Son of Man" twice in Mark's gospel. First, when Jesus heals the paralyzed man and says, "The Son of Man has authority on earth to forgive sins" (Mark 2:10). Second, when Jesus says, "The Son of Man is Lord even of the Sabbath" (v. 28). Both times, Jesus is claiming incredible authority! This fits with Daniel's vision in the Old Testament of one "like a son of man" who came on the clouds of heaven and was given a universal, everlasting kingdom by God Himself (Daniel 7:13–14).

Why is it surprising that the "elders, the chief priests and the teachers of the law" would reject God's promised King?

_____

_____

_____

At the end of verse 31, what amazing thing does Jesus say will happen to the Son of Man?

_____

_____

_____

In verse 32, how does Peter react to Jesus' teaching?

_____

_____

_____

➦**FUN FACT:** As we saw on Day 13, when Jesus rebukes the wind and calms the storm, to rebuke someone means to express strong disapproval of what they are saying or doing.

What does Jesus call Peter in response to this in verse 33?

_____

_____

_____

What does Jesus say Peter is doing (v. 33)?

_____

_____

_____

⇒ FUN FACT: In Mark 1:12, we heard that Jesus was tempted by Satan for forty days in the wilderness. In Matthew's gospel we find out that Satan shows Jesus all the kingdoms of the world and says he would give Jesus those kingdoms if Jesus would bow down and worship him (Matthew 4:8–9). Jesus tells Satan to go away. Jesus is only going to worship God, and He knows that the way He is going to get His kingdom is by dying.

Peter was one of Jesus' closest friends. Yesterday, we heard him declaring that Jesus is the Messiah. How do you think Peter felt when Jesus called him "Satan"?

_____

_____

_____

Jesus says He's the King who has come to die. How is this different from how we might expect a king to act?

_____

_____

_____

The Jews were hoping for a king who would kick the Romans out. How does Jesus predicting His death and resurrection show He's come to fight a different battle?

_____

_____

_____

 PRAY: Thank God that He sent Jesus to die for us, so we could be forgiven for our sins, and to rise again, so we can live with Him forever even after we die too.

JESUS CALLS US TO COME AND DIE

Today, a lot of people wear crosses around their necks, like jewelry. But in Jesus' day, no one would have dreamed of doing that. The cross was the most terrible instrument of torture—the worst way anyone could imagine dying! The Romans crucified people in public, to show everyone what would happen to anyone who stood up against the power of Rome. In our passage today, we'll see that Jesus didn't just predict that He would die. He predicted He'd be crucified. What's more, He called His followers to die that way too.

Read Mark 8:34–9:1

What two groups of people is Jesus talking to at the beginning of verse 34?

_____

_____

_____

In verse 34, Jesus says anyone who wants to follow Him must do three things. Write them down below:

1. deny _____

2. take up _____

3. follow _____

➨**SERIOUS FACT:** People who were going to be crucified were forced to carry their own crosses on the way to the place where they'd be killed. Jesus literally took up a cross and died for us, and many Christians around the world today live in countries where they could be killed for following Jesus.

In smaller ways, how might we suffer for sharing the gospel with people at school, in our neighborhood, or in our family?

_____

_____

_____

What does Jesus say to His disciples and the crowd in verse 35?

_____

_____

_____

Jesus claims that anyone who loses their life for His sake will find it. How is that more evidence that God's kingdom turns everything upside down and inside out?

_____

_____

_____

What question does Jesus ask in verse 36?

_____

_____

_____

✦FUN FACT: "Forfeit" means lose. So, Jesus is asking, "What's the point of getting everything you want but losing your soul?" If we don't put our trust in Jesus, we might get everything we want in this life—like money, success, an amazing husband or wife, a loving family, fame, or beauty—but in the end, we'll face God's judgment for our sin.

What question does Jesus ask in verse 37?

_____

_____

_____

➡AMAZING FACT: There's *nothing* we could give in exchange for our soul, but Jesus gave His own life in exchange for ours when He died on the cross! He paid the price for us, so we could live eternally with Him!

How do you feel, knowing that Jesus gave His life for you?

What warning does Jesus give in verse 38?

Why might we be ashamed of following Jesus in front of our friends?

What prediction does Jesus make in chapter 9, verse 1?

➡FUN FACT: Some experts think Jesus was talking about a revelation of His glory (we'll read about that tomorrow). Others think Jesus meant His resurrection, which proved He really is God's promised King, or the day God poured out His Spirit on His disciples (Acts 2). Still others think Jesus was talking about the final judgment day when He will come back to earth. We don't know exactly what Jesus meant, but we do know that His kingdom has already started and that one day He will come to rule forevermore.

PRAY: Thank God that Jesus died for you. Ask Him to help you follow Jesus, even when it's really hard—like when you lose friends for being a Christian or miss out on things you really want. Pray that Jesus would help you believe His promise that whoever loses their life for Him will find it.

JESUS IS REVEALED
AS GOD'S SON (AGAIN)!

Think of your favorite superhero movie. In most of them, the hero just looks like an ordinary guy or girl until we suddenly see them show their superpowers. So far in Mark, we've seen Jesus do amazing things— like healing people, walking on water, and feeding thousands with a few loaves of bread. But all along, He's *looked* just like a regular guy. In our passage today, we get a glimpse of Jesus looking not so ordinary!

Read Mark 9:2–13

In verse 2, who did Jesus take with Him, and where did they go?

What does Mark say happened to Jesus in verses 2–3?

➥*FUN FACT:* The word "transfigured" means changed. When Matthew describes this moment, he says that Jesus' face "shone like the sun" (Matthew 17:2).

What two other people appeared and talked with Jesus in verse 4?

➔FUN FACT: Moses and Elijah would have made Jews of Jesus' day think of the law (Moses) and the prophets (Elijah). So, Jesus meeting with them both was sort of like the whole Old Testament Scripture showing up!

In verses 5–6, what does Peter suggest they do and why?

What happens in verse 7?

➔FUN FACT: When Jesus was baptized, a voice came from heaven, saying, "You are my Son, whom I love; with you I am well pleased" (Mark 1:11). Now, at the transfiguration, God's voice speaks again, saying, "This is my Son, whom I love. Listen to him!"

As they were coming down the mountain (v. 9), what instructions did Jesus give to Peter, James, and John?

How does Jesus' instruction here remind you of His instruction to His disciples after Peter said, "You are the Messiah!"? (See Day 27.)

What are Peter, James, and John wondering about in verse 10?

✦FUN FACT: Many Jews in Jesus' day believed that at the final judgment day, God would raise His people from the dead. But they had no idea that He would raise Jesus from the dead in their own time.

What do they ask Jesus in verse 11?

_____

_____

_____

Because of Malachi's prophecy, many Jews believed Elijah would return before the Messiah. Does Jesus agree or disagree with this belief (v. 12)?

_____

_____

_____

✦FUN FACT: At the beginning of his gospel, Mark applies a prophecy about Elijah to John the Baptist. John comes before Jesus to prepare the way. He even dresses like Elijah (see 2 Kings 1:8 and Mark 1:6). But instead of being taken up into heaven, like Elijah, John is beheaded by Herod.

What does Jesus say happened to the new Elijah (i.e., John the Baptist) in verse 13?

_____

_____

_____

In verse 12, Jesus tells His disciples again that the Son of Man must suffer much and be rejected. Why do you think He keeps reminding them of this?

_____

_____

_____

We've just seen Jesus being revealed in His glory on a mountaintop and God's voice speaking from heaven. Now He's teaching again that He must die. How is this another example of how God's kingdom turns things upside down?

_____

_____

_____

 PRAY: Praise Jesus that He is greater than any imaginary superhero and that He chose to use His power to save us by dying in our place and rising again.

JESUS MEETS A MAN WHO STRUGGLES TO BELIEVE

Do you ever wish you had more faith in Jesus? Maybe you look at other people and they seem to have an easier time believing Jesus truly is the Son of God who died for them. Sometimes, you find it really hard to trust that Jesus is the King of all the universe. Today, we'll meet a man who did believe in Jesus, but also knew he needed help with his unbelief.

Read Mark 9:14–29

When Jesus, Peter, James, and John came down from the mountain, who did they find there (v. 14)?

_____

_____

_____

How did the people react when they saw Jesus (v. 15)?

_____

_____

_____

What question did Jesus ask (v. 16)?

_____

_____

_____

Who answered (v. 17)?

_____

_____

_____

This dad had tried to bring his son to Jesus, but as Jesus wasn't there, he asked the disciples to drive out the spirit. Were His disciples able to help (v. 18)?

_____

_____

_____

How does Jesus describe the generation of people around Him (v. 19)?

_____

_____

_____

➤**FUN FACT:** A generation is a group of people who are roughly the same age. In our culture, we give names to different generations. If you were born in 2012 or earlier, you're classed as "Gen Z." If you were born after 2012, you're "Gen Alpha." Jesus calls His generation "Gen Unbelieving!"

Jesus is frustrated by the unbelief of those around Him, but He wants to help the boy. What did the spirit do to the boy when he saw Jesus (v. 20)?

_____

_____

_____

How long did the boy's father say his son had been suffering like this (v. 21)?

_____

_____

_____

The man says to Jesus, "If you can do anything, take pity on us and help" (v. 22). How does Jesus respond (v. 23)?

_____

_____

_____

How does the man respond to Jesus (v. 24)?

_____

_____

_____

✦**FUN FACT:** This man's response has become very famous because it expresses how many Christians feel. We _do_ believe in Jesus. But we also know how weak our faith can be and how much we need Jesus to help us believe. If that's how you feel sometimes, you're not alone!

What does Jesus do after the man says he believes and asks for help with his unbelief (v. 25)?

_____

_____

_____

What happens to the boy when the spirit comes out of him (v. 26)?

_____

_____

_____

What did Jesus do to the boy who looked like he was dead (v. 27)?

_____

_____

_____

What did the disciples ask Jesus when they were alone with Him (v. 28)?

_____

_____

_____

How did Jesus respond (v. 29)?

_____

_____

_____

Prayer is powerful, so let's pray!

 PRAY: If you're trusting in Jesus, thank Him for your belief and ask Him to help you in the times when you struggle to believe He really is the Son of God and that He can do truly incredible things. If you don't think you're trusting in Jesus yet, ask Him to help you with your unbelief and give you faith in Him!

JESUS TURNS EVERYTHING UPSIDE DOWN

If you like basketball, you'll know that Michael Jordan is the GOAT. This doesn't mean that he's a furry animal. It means he's the greatest basketball player of all time. Fans of different sports debate who is the GOAT of each one. And even if you don't like sports, you might care about the GOAT of your favorite kind of music or dance. But in our passage today, Jesus turns our natural ideas of greatness, power, and status on their heads.

Read Mark 9:30–37

Where did Jesus and His disciples go (v. 30)?

Jesus was raised in Galilee, and He started His public ministry there, but Mark tells us that this time He wanted to keep a low profile. Why (v. 31)?

What was Jesus teaching His disciples (v. 31)?

→**FUN FACT:** This is the second time since Peter recognizes Jesus as the Messiah that Jesus has predicted His death and resurrection (see Mark 8:31–32).

How did the disciples respond to Jesus teaching them that He would be killed and raised to life (v. 32)?

_____

_____

_____

What did Jesus ask them when they got to Capernaum—the fishing village in Galilee where Jesus had begun His public ministry (v. 33)?

_____

_____

_____

How did His disciples respond to Jesus' question (v. 34)?

_____

_____

_____

Why didn't the disciples answer Jesus (v. 34)?

_____

_____

_____

�+FUN FACT: Jesus knows what His disciples have been talking about, just like He knew what the teachers of the law were thinking when He told the paralyzed man his sins were forgiven (Mark 2:6–8).

What does Jesus say to His disciples in response to their argument about which of them was the greatest (v. 35)?

_____

_____

_____

How is Jesus' teaching here the opposite of what we might normally expect?

_____

_____

_____

✦**FUN FACT:** In Jesus' day, many people worked as servants or even slaves. They were seen as much less important than the people they were serving. But Jesus turns this upside down and says that anyone who wants to be important must be the servant of everyone else.

What did Jesus do next (v. 36)?

_____

_____

_____

What does Jesus say about little children (v. 37)?

_____

_____

_____

✦**FUN FACT:** Today, we wouldn't think it was strange for an important person to spend time with a little child. But at the time when Jesus was teaching, children were seen as insignificant. Important people would not bend down and welcome a child. But Jesus did, and He said that's how His followers should act as well.

Do you ever feel insignificant because of your age?

_____

_____

_____

How does Jesus' teaching here help you think differently about yourself?

_____

_____

_____

PRAY: Thank Jesus that He cares about the people who seem least important. Ask Him to help you be the kind of person who is more focused on serving others than on getting ahead yourself.

NOTHING IS MORE IMPORTANT THAN ENTERING GOD'S KINGDOM

Do you remember what Jesus said before He healed the paralyzed man? "Son, your sins are forgiven!" (Mark 2:5). The man probably thought that being unable to walk was his main problem. But Jesus seemed to think that the man having his sins forgiven was even more important than being able to walk. In today's passage, we'll hear Jesus say this clearly: entering God's kingdom is much more important than being able to walk.

Read Mark 9:38–50

In verse 28, John tells Jesus that the disciples had seen a man driving out demons in Jesus' name, and they told the man to stop. How does Jesus respond (v. 39)?

In verse 40, Jesus divides everyone into two groups: people who are for Him and people who are against Him. What example does Jesus give of how someone might show they were on Jesus' side (v. 41)?

Jesus says that anyone who helps one of His disciples will be rewarded (Mark 9:41). What does He say about anyone who causes one of the little ones who believe in Him to stumble (v. 42)?

_____

_____

_____

➡**FUN FACT:** We don't know if Jesus just means children when He says "these little ones" or if He is talking about all His followers. But either way, He cares so much about His followers that if someone trips them up on their way into God's kingdom, Jesus says it would be better for that person to drown.

In verse 43, Jesus says something even more shocking. What does he say you should do if your hand causes you to stumble?

_____

_____

_____

Why does Jesus say it is better to lose one of your hands than to trip up and stop following Him (v. 44)?

_____

_____

_____

What other body parts does Jesus say you'd be better to lose than to stop following Him (vv. 45–47)?

_____

_____

_____

➡**SERIOUS FACT:** Jesus' point here is not that we should literally cut off our body parts, because it's not our feet or hands or eyes that cause us to sin. As He explained in Mark 7:21–23, our problem is our heart, and we can't cut that out! Only Jesus' death on the cross can deal with our sin. But Jesus is showing how important it is that we keep following Him—more important than being able to walk or see.

What two pictures does Jesus use to describe hell in verse 48?

SERIOUS FACT: Throughout Mark's gospel, we've seen Jesus' kindness and compassion. We've seen Him healing people and forgiving them. But here we see Jesus talking very seriously about God's judgment. People who don't put their trust in Jesus and believe He died and rose again for them will one day face that judgment.

What would you do if someone who you knew was really kind warned you that a terrible fire was coming and you had to come with them to get to safety now?

In verse 50, Jesus uses a metaphor, or word picture, of salt. In Matthew's gospel, Jesus uses the same metaphor to talk about the distinctive way in which His followers should live (Matthew 5:13). What characteristic of His followers does Jesus highlight at the end of verse 50?

PRAY: Thank Jesus that He died on the cross so that you and I could enter God's kingdom instead of facing God's judgment. Pray for a friend or family member, who is not yet trusting in Jesus, that he or she would recognize who Jesus is and come to Him for forgiveness and eternal life.

DAY
34

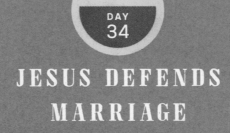

JESUS DEFENDS MARRIAGE

Today's passage is on a very painful subject. You might have experienced divorce in your own family, or maybe you worry that your parents could get divorced. Divorce is so painful because marriage is so precious. As Jesus explains, when a man and a woman marry, God makes them "one flesh." So, divorce is like tearing your body apart.

Read Mark 10:1–12

Jesus was in Galilee, where He grew up, but now He goes down south to Judea. As we'll see in the next few days, He's heading to Jerusalem. Who meets Him in verse 2, and what do they ask?

Jesus responds with a question. What does He ask them?

How do the Pharisees answer Jesus' question?

➔***NOT-SO-FUN FACT:*** In Jesus' day, it was easy for a man to divorce his wife, and it was really hard on the woman and her children if that happened because they likely depended on the man for their food and housing.

Why does Jesus say that Moses allowed divorce (v. 5)?

_____

_____

_____

What does Jesus say happened when God first created humans (v. 6)?

_____

⇥FUN FACT: Jesus is quoting from the first chapter of the Bible: "So God created mankind in his own image, in the image of God he created them; male and female he created them" (Genesis 1:27). Next, He quotes from the second chapter, when God makes the first woman out of the first man's side. The man says, "This is now bone of my bones and flesh of my flesh; she shall be called 'woman,' for she was taken out of man." The author of Genesis adds: "That is why a man leaves his father and mother and is united to his wife, and they become one flesh" (Genesis 2:23–24).

What comment does Jesus add to the quote from Genesis in Mark 10:8–9?

_____

_____

In our culture today, many people see marriage as mostly about two people coming together to make each other happy. So, if the relationship stops making one of the people happy, it makes sense to them to end the marriage. But Jesus has a different view. Who does Jesus say joins people together in marriage (v. 9)?

_____

_____

➥FUN FACT: As we saw on Day 7, the apostle Paul explains that marriage is a signpost to Jesus' love for us. He says that husbands are to love their wives just like Christ loved the church and gave Himself up for her on the cross.

If marriage, at its best, is a picture of Jesus' love for us, how seriously should we take marriage?

_____

_____

_____

If marriage, at its best, is a picture of Jesus' love for us, how does that help us see that getting married is not the point of our lives, but Jesus is?

_____

_____

_____

In verses 11–12, what does Jesus say happens if someone gets divorced and marries someone else?

_____

_____

_____

➔**SERIOUS FACT:** In Matthew, Jesus says that it's okay to divorce your wife or husband if they have cheated on you (Matthew 19:9). Some people get abandoned and don't have a choice. Others are abused by their husband or wife and have to leave. But Jesus is clear that marriage makes two people one and that breaking up a marriage is incredibly serious. This is hard for us to hear, as so many Christians today have divorced. Many of Jesus' teachings are hard for us to hear, as they call out our sin. But Jesus also loves sinners. In John, Jesus has His longest conversation with a woman who had been married five times and was now living with a man she wasn't married to (John 4:1–26).

PRAY: If your parents are married, pray that God would help them be a picture of Jesus' love for His church. If they are divorced or never got married to begin with, pray for God's help and healing for them.

JESUS WELCOMES CHILDREN

There are three children in our family: Miranda is twelve, Eliza is ten, and Luke is four. We all love Luke very much. But he can also be extremely difficult! It's hard work caring for a little kid, and sometimes none of us want to play with him or read to him or pay attention to him because we're busy with other things. In our passage today, Jesus' disciples think Jesus must be much too busy to bother with some little kids. But the disciples are completely wrong.

Read Mark 10:13–16

In verse 13, what were people doing and why?

_____

_____

_____

How did Jesus' disciples respond (v. 13)?

_____

_____

_____

How did Jesus feel when He saw His disciples telling people off for bringing their little children to Him (v. 14)?

_____

_____

_____

In verse 14, what did Jesus say His disciples should do and why?

_____

_____

_____

⇥✦FUN FACT: This Bible passage changed the way that children were seen. As we saw on Day 32, little kids in Jesus' day were seen as insignificant. They were treated more like possessions than like people. But Jesus took a very different view, and this is the main reason why people see babies and little children as full humans today.

What does Jesus say about the kingdom of God in verse 15?

_____

_____

_____

How do little children react when you give them a gift?

_____

_____

How could we be more like little children in our response to Jesus' offer of forgiveness and eternal life with Him?

_____

_____

_____

Adults sometimes act like kids aren't old enough yet to be real disciples of Jesus. How does this passage help us see that in Jesus' upside-down kingdom, children don't have to have faith like an adult, but adults have to have faith like a child?

_____

_____

_____

What did Jesus do for the children who had been brought to Him (v. 16)?

_____

_____

_____

Imagine you were one of those children Jesus took in His arms and blessed. How do you think you would feel?

_____

_____

➤**AMAZING FACT:** If you are trusting in Jesus today, you are just like one of those little children! He's got you wrapped up in His arms, and He's speaking God's blessing over you all the time. Any time you feel alone or sad or hurt or afraid, Jesus is right there with you, holding you in His arms. He loves you so much that He died for you. You are incredibly important to Him!

If you have a little brother or sister, how does this story help you think differently about him or her?

_____

_____

_____

What could you do to help your little brother or sister learn about Jesus and receive His kingdom?

_____

_____

_____

PRAY: Thank God that Jesus is holding you in His arms and blessing you. Thank Him that Jesus will never let go of you. If you have a little brother or sister, pray for him or her to recognize who Jesus is and receive His offer of forgiveness and eternal life.

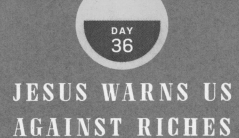

JESUS WARNS US AGAINST RICHES

A lot of people in our culture want to be rich. Having lots of money makes us humans feel successful and important. Maybe you're hoping you'll be rich when you grow up! But in our passage today, we'll see that instead of being a mark of a successful life, having lots of money can actually lead people to fail at the only thing that matters in the end: entering God's kingdom.

Read Mark 10:17–31

In verse 17, what did the man do and what question did he ask?

How did Jesus respond at first (v. 18)?

➡✦*FUN FACT:* Jesus often answers a question with another question. Here, He makes the point that only God is really, truly good. Jesus isn't saying that He *isn't* God. He's making the man think!

In verse 19, Jesus points the man back to the famous Ten Commandments that God gave Moses. How many of the Ten Commandments
does He quote?

⇥FUN FACT: The first four commandments relate to worshiping God. Jesus skips
these and only quotes the ones that relate to how we treat other people.

What does the man say he has done (v. 20)?

Does it seem like the man thinks he is basically good?

How does Jesus feel about the man (v. 21)?

What does Jesus tell the man to do at the beginning of verse 21?

Why does Jesus say he should sell everything and give to the poor (v. 21)?

_____

_____

_____

What else does Jesus say the man must do (v. 21)?

_____

_____

_____

✦**FUN FACT:** Instead of quoting the commandments on how we treat God, Jesus tells the man to follow Him. Jesus says only God is good. Now, He steps into God's shoes and tells the man that to have eternal life he must follow Him.

How does the man react to Jesus' command and why (v. 22)?

_____

_____

_____

What does Jesus say once the rich man has left (v. 23)?

_____

_____

_____

The disciples are shocked by Jesus' words. They probably thought that rich people were especially blessed by God. But Jesus makes His point even more dramatically!

What does He say is easier than a rich man to entering God's kingdom (v. 25)?

_____

_____

_____

The disciples are even more shocked and wonder who can be saved. How does Jesus respond (v. 27)?

⇒✦FUN FACT: It's just as impossible for any of us to be saved as for a great big camel to squeeze through the tiny hole in a needle. But Jesus did the impossible: He's God, yet He became a man to die on the cross in our place.

Peter points out that he has left everything to follow Jesus. What does Jesus say that people who leave everything to follow Him will get (vv. 29–30)?

How does Jesus summarize His upside-down kingdom in verse 31?

PRAY: Thank God He sent Jesus so we could have eternal life with Him. Ask God to help you not be drawn to money and away from Him as you grow up.

JESUS PREDICTS HIS DEATH A THIRD TIME

In *Harry Potter and the Deathly Hallows*, Harry walks toward his death. The evil Voldemort has demanded Harry come and face him, or Voldemort will kill all Harry's friends. So, Harry walks to the Forbidden Forest where Voldemort is waiting. In our passage today, Jesus walks deliberately toward His death as well. But instead of the Forbidden Forest, He's going to Jerusalem.

Read Mark 10:32–34

Where was Jesus leading His disciples toward (v. 32)?

_____

_____

How did the disciples feel about Jesus' choice to go to Jerusalem (v. 32)?

_____

_____

_____

How did the others who were following Jesus feel (v. 32)?

_____

_____

_____

➼**IMPORTANT FACT:** Jerusalem was the capital city of Judea. People went to Jerusalem to visit the temple where they could worship God with sacrifices and prayer. But Jesus' disciples know it's dangerous for Jesus to go to Jerusalem at this point because the religious leaders want to kill Him.

Who does Jesus take aside in verse 32?

_____

_____

Who does Jesus say He will be handed over to in Jerusalem (v. 33)?

_____

_____

What does Jesus say the chief priests and the teachers of the law will do to Him (v. 33)?

_____

_____

➡️**IMPORTANT FACT:** To condemn someone to death means to judge that they deserve to be executed. When Jesus says "the Gentiles" here, He means the Romans who were ruling over the Jews at the time.

What four details does Jesus give about what the Romans will do to Him (v. 34)?

_____

_____

_____

➡️**SAD FACT:** Before the Romans crucified people, they often flogged them—which means to beat someone severely with a whip.

How do these details show that Jesus is ready not only to be killed but also to be shamed and humiliated for our sakes?

_____

_____

_____

What does Jesus say will happen three days after He's been killed (v. 34)?

_____

_____

_____

➜**IMPORTANT FACT:** This is the third time in Mark's gospel that Jesus has predicted His death and resurrection. But this time, He's on His way to Jerusalem and preparing His disciples in detail for what's going to happen to Him.

What does Jesus' ability to predict exactly what's going to happen to Him show us about His control?

_____

_____

_____

How do you think you would have felt if you had been one of Jesus' first disciples hearing this?

_____

_____

_____

As we'll see in our study tomorrow, Jesus' disciples still didn't understand what Jesus was saying to them and that His kingdom was all upside down. It's really hard for us to grasp that too!

_____

_____

_____

PRAY: Thank Jesus that He was willing to go to Jerusalem to be mocked and spat on and beaten up and killed for you. Praise Him that He rose again and beat death, so that you can live with Him forever.

JESUS CAME TO SERVE
AND GIVE HIS LIFE

The first time Jesus told His disciples He was going to be rejected and killed, Peter tried to talk Him out of it (Mark 8:32). The second time Jesus taught His disciples He was going to be rejected and killed, His disciples started arguing about which of them was the greatest (Mark 9:34). Yesterday, we looked at the third time Jesus predicted His death, and today we'll see that once again, His disciples react by trying to defend their own importance.

Read Mark 10:35–45

In verse 35, who came to Jesus with a request?

_____

_____

What was their request (v. 37)?

_____

_____

_____

➥**FUN FACT:** Sitting next to a king on his right was the place of greatest honor and authority. That spot would often be taken by the son and heir of the king or by his top adviser. Sitting on the king's left would be the next best place.

How does Jesus respond to this request at the beginning of verse 38?

_____

_____

_____

What two questions does Jesus ask them (v. 38)?

_____

_____

_____

➥**IMPORTANT FACT:** In the Old Testament, the cup of the Lord symbolized His judgment on sin. Drinking that cup meant facing terrible suffering. When Jesus talks about baptism here, He is also using it as a picture of His suffering and death. He will come into His glory by going to the cross.

How do James and John respond to Jesus' questions (v. 39)?

_____

_____

_____

How does Jesus respond in verse 39?

_____

_____

_____

➥**IMPORTANT FACT:** Later in Mark, we'll see Jesus sharing a special cup with His disciples (Mark 14:23–24). We also know that James and John both went on to suffer for their faith in Jesus. In fact, we read about James being executed in Acts 12:1–2. In one sense, they would share in Jesus' suffering. But Jesus says He cannot give James and John the places they have asked for.

How do the other disciples react when they hear about James and John's request (v. 41)?

_____

_____

_____

To be "indignant" means to be annoyed or angry because you think you've been treated unfairly.

In response, Jesus calls them together to teach them. How does Jesus describe how the rulers of the Gentiles act (v. 42)?

_____

_____

_____

How does Jesus say that leaders in His kingdom must be different (vv. 43–44)?

_____

_____

_____

Why does Jesus say that leaders in His kingdom must serve everyone else, not expect everyone else to serve them (v. 45)?

_____

_____

_____

➜**FUN FACT:** The word "ransom" means a payment to get someone set free. The original Greek word was often used to describe a payment made to free a slave. Jesus is the Son of Man—the rightful ruler over all the world—but He didn't come to be served. He came to serve and to give His life as a payment for our freedom.

Mark 10:45 is an extremely important verse in Mark's gospel. Write it down and see if you can memorize it!

"For even the Son of Man did not come to be served, but to serve, and to give his life as a ransom for many." (Mark 10:45)

Jesus is the GOAT. But He came not to be served but to serve, and to give His life for us!

 PRAY: Praise Jesus that He was willing to serve us by dying in our place. Pray that He would help you not to be like James and John, who wanted the top spots in His kingdom, but instead to be like Jesus Himself, who was willing to serve others.

JESUS HEALS ANOTHER BLIND MAN

Most people have five senses: sight, hearing, touch, taste, and smell. When someone loses one sense, they often get really good at using the others. For example, many deaf people can tell what other people are saying by lip reading, while many blind people use touch to read. Today, we'll meet a blind man who can see who Jesus is, when many seeing people could not.

Read Mark 10:46–52

What city did Jesus and His disciples arrive at in verse 46?

_____

_____

Who was sitting by the road as Jesus, His disciples, and the crowd were leaving (v. 46)?

_____

_____

➛✦FUN FACT: Bartimaeus is the only healed person in Mark's gospel whose name we know! Often, when the Gospels tell us someone's name, it's because they are one of the eyewitnesses whose story the author is writing down for us or because they were known to the early Christians. Here, it's possible that both Bartimaeus and his father, Timaeus, were known to the church.

What was Bartimaeus doing (v. 46)?

_____

_____

_____

What did he do when he heard that Jesus was coming by (v. 47)?

_____

_____

How did people respond when they heard Bartimaeus shouting this (v. 48)?

_____

_____

What did Bartimaeus do when people told him to be quiet (v. 48)?

_____

_____

What did Jesus do when He heard Bartimaeus calling out to Him (v. 49)?

_____

_____

What did Bartimaeus do when he heard that Jesus had called for him (v. 50)?

_____

_____

What did Jesus ask Bartimaeus (v. 51)?

_____

_____

How did Bartimaeus answer (v. 51)?

_____

_____

What does Jesus tell Bartimaeus (v. 52)?

_____

_____

What happened to Bartimaeus and what did he do in response (v. 52)?

_____

_____

_____

➔**FUN FACT:** Right before Peter recognized that Jesus was the Messiah, Jesus healed a blind man (Mark 8:22–26). In this passage, it's the blind man himself who recognizes Jesus as the Messiah, then calls Him "Son of David." The man can see who Jesus is, even though he's blind, while the Pharisees and chief priests and teachers of the law could not see who Jesus was at all.

How does Bartimaeus' response to Jesus throughout this story teach us about how we should respond to Jesus?

_____

_____

_____

How does this story show us Jesus serving others like He said He'd come to do?

_____

_____

_____

See if you can still remember yesterday's memory verse! Look back at Mark 10:45 if you need a reminder.

 PRAY: Praise God that He sent Jesus to be the great King, who brings healing to the sick and hope to the poor. Pray that He would help you feel like Bartimaeus: eager to see Jesus as the King, to bring your needs to Him, and to follow Him.

Well done! You've made it to the end of Act 4!

JESUS ENTERS

JERUSALEM

AS KING

At last, at the beginning of Act 5, Jesus rides into Jerusalem as King. He goes straight to the temple and starts acting like He owns the place! The religious leaders question His right to do this, but they don't dare to act against Him yet, because the crowds are following Him. Then Jesus tells a parable that calls out the chief priests, teachers of the law, and elders, and they look for a way to arrest Him.

The religious leaders really don't want Jesus to be king. The Pharisees and Herodians try to trap Jesus by asking if they should pay taxes to Caesar, but Jesus cleverly shows that God is more important than the Roman emperor. Then, another Jewish group, known as the Sadducees, try to catch Jesus out on His belief in resurrection, but they fail as well. Finally, a teacher of the law asks Jesus what's the most important commandment, and Jesus shows that loving God comes first and loving others as ourselves comes second. But He's not done.

Jesus shows that the Messiah is greater than King David and that a poor widow's offering is greater than all the money the rich are giving to the temple. Then, He predicts the destruction of the temple, which takes place in AD 70, and warns His disciples about the day when He will come again in glory to judge.

Jesus is the mighty King. But as we'll see in Act 6, He's the King who has come to die.

Act 1: Mark 1–2 **JESUS IS GOD'S PROMISED KING**	
Act 2: Mark 3–5 **JESUS STARTS HIS KINGDOM FAMILY**	**Act 5: Mark 11–13** **JESUS ENTERS JERUSALEM AS KING**
Act 3: Mark 6–8:26 **JESUS GROWS HIS KINGDOM FAMILY**	**Act 4: Mark 8:27–10:52** **JESUS TURNS GOD'S KINGDOM UPSIDE DOWN**

JESUS RIDES INTO JERUSALEM AS KING

In The Lord of the Rings, when Aragorn is finally crowned king of Gondor, Tolkien writes, "All that beheld him gazed in silence, for it seemed to them that he was revealed to them now for the first time. Tall as the sea-kings of old, he stood above all that were near; ancient of days he seemed and yet in the flower of manhood; and wisdom sat upon his brow, and strength and healing were in his hands, and a light was about him."[3] Today, we'll read about Jesus entering Jerusalem as its humble but glorious King.

Read Mark 11:1–11

As He was nearing Jerusalem, what did Jesus send two disciples to get (v. 2)?

⁑**FUN FACT:** The word translated "colt" means a young horse or donkey. The prophet Zechariah prophesies about God's promised King like this:

> Rejoice greatly, Daughter Zion!
> Shout, Daughter Jerusalem!
> See, your king comes to you,
> righteous and victorious,
> lowly and riding on a donkey,
> on a colt, the foal of a donkey. (Zechariah 9:9)

What did Jesus tell His disciples to say if someone asked why they were untying the colt (v. 3)?

_____

_____

What did the disciples do to the colt when they'd brought it to Jesus (v. 7)?

_____

_____

_____

What did Jesus do (v. 7)?

_____

_____

_____

What did lots of people do to the road in front of Jesus (v. 8)?

_____

_____

➦**FUN FACT:** In our culture, we might roll out a red carpet in front of someone super important before they walk down the aisle. People laying down branches they had cut from the fields and putting their cloaks on the road in front of Jesus would have been similar to that.

What were the people around Jesus shouting in verse 9?

_____

_____

_____

➦**FUN FACT:** "Hosanna" means "Save now!" and was shouted to God. For example, in Psalm 118, we read, "LORD, save us! LORD, grant us success! Blessed is he who comes in the name of the LORD!" (Psalm 118:25–26).

How does the crowd shouting "Hosanna" line up with Jesus' claim that He came not to be served but to serve and give His life as a ransom for many?

_____

_____

_____

What are people shouting out in verse 10?

_____

_____

_____

How does this show that Jesus was being welcomed as the Messiah?

_____

_____

_____

➔**FUN FACT:** When Luke tells this story, he records the Pharisees telling Jesus to rebuke His disciples for proclaiming that He's the Messiah. Jesus responds, "I tell you, if they keep quiet, the stones will cry out" (Luke 19:40).

Where does Jesus go when He's gone into Jerusalem (v. 11)?

_____

_____

_____

Why did He leave again (v. 11)?

_____

_____

_____

Throughout Mark's gospel, we've seen Jesus try to keep people quiet when they start to realize who He is. But today, we see Him entering Jerusalem with crowds proclaiming that He's God's long-promised King.

Why do you think Jesus is going public at last?

Praise Jesus that He is God's promised King and that He used His power to save. Pray that you would have courage to tell your friends and family that Jesus is the King who came to save them.

JESUS ACTS LIKE HE OWNS THE TEMPLE

We only have one story in the Bible from when Jesus was about your age. When Jesus was twelve, Mary and Joseph took Him to Jerusalem for the Passover festival, just as they did every year. When the festival was over, His family headed home to Nazareth. But after the first day's journey, they realized Jesus wasn't with them. So, they went back to Jerusalem to search for Him. Three days later, they found Him in the temple courts, listening to the teachers and asking them questions. When His mother asked Him why He'd treated His parents like that, Jesus replied, "Didn't you know I had to be in my Father's house?" (Luke 2:49). Today, we'll see Jesus going into His Father's house and acting like He owns the place—because He does!

Read Mark 11:12–21

How did Jesus feel on His way from Bethany to Jerusalem (v. 12)?

What did Jesus do when He found there were no figs on the fig tree yet (v. 14)?

✦FUN FACT: The prophets sometimes used fig trees as pictures when they warned about God's judgment on Israel. Like Israel, this literal fig tree isn't ready for Jesus when He comes, so He speaks judgment on it. Likewise, when Jesus comes to the temple, the people there aren't ready for Him.

What did Jesus do when He entered the temple courts (vv. 15–16)?

_____

_____

_____

➥**FUN FACT:** One of the things God's people were commanded to do at the temple was make sacrifices. So, it was important that people could buy animals for sacrifice near the temple. But the people selling animals and birds for sacrifice have set up shop in the temple itself, very likely in the part known as the Court of the Gentiles, which was the only place where non-Jews could worship.

How does Jesus explain why He is doing this in verse 17?

_____

_____

_____

➥**FUN FACT:** Jesus quotes from two Old Testament prophets. The first quotation is from Isaiah, when God is talking about how He will include Gentiles who put their trust in Him. God says:

> "These I will bring to my holy mountain
>   and give them joy in my house of prayer.
> Their burnt offerings and sacrifices
>   will be accepted on my altar;
> for my house will be called
>   a house of prayer for all nations." (Isaiah 56:7)

The second quotation is from Jeremiah, where God says about His temple, "Has this house, which bears my Name, become a den of robbers to you?" (Jeremiah 7:11).

What did Jesus want His Father's house to be used for instead of trading (v. 17)?

_____

_____

_____

How do the chief priests and teachers of the law react to Jesus driving traders out of the temple and speaking these words of judgment (v. 18)?

_____

_____

_____

How does the reaction of the chief priests and teachers of the law show that Jesus' prediction in Mark 10:33 was going to come true?

_____

_____

_____

When Jesus and His disciples were heading back to Jerusalem the next morning, what did they see had happened (v. 20)?

_____

_____

_____

How does the withering of this fig tree show the power of Jesus' judgment?

_____

_____

_____

PRAY: Praise God that He has opened up His kingdom to anyone who comes to Him, whether they are Jewish or not. Pray for a friend or family member who does not yet trust in Jesus, that they would turn and trust in Him and be ready for when Jesus comes again.

JESUS SAYS PRAYER CAN MOVE MOUNTAINS

What's the biggest prayer you've ever prayed? Maybe you prayed for someone you love who was sick to get well, or for help when you were scared, or for a friend to start following Jesus. Yesterday, we saw Jesus throwing traders out of the temple because He wanted it to be a house of prayer. Today, we'll see how powerful Jesus says prayer is.

Read Mark 11:22–25

What does Jesus tell His disciples to do in verse 22?

_____

_____

_____

What amazing claim does Jesus make in verse 23?

_____

_____

_____

➔**FUN FACT:** Jesus sometimes teaches via hyperbole (pronounced hy-PER-bo-lee), which means an extreme statement not intended to be taken literally. Jesus is giving an extreme example of prayer. It's impossible for a human being to tell a mountain what to do and for the mountain to obey, just as it's impossible for a camel to squeeze through the eye of a needle (Mark 10:25). But nothing is impossible for God (Mark 10:27)!

Do you think Jesus meant for His disciples to start commanding mountains to throw themselves into the sea?

_____

_____

How does Jesus' extreme example give us encouragement to pray big prayers and trust God's power to act?

_____

_____

_____

What makes it hard for you to pray and trust God?

_____

_____

_____

➔**FUN FACT:** Sometimes God does not answer our prayers in the way we want because He has a better plan. For example, the apostle Paul prayed three times for God to take away his suffering, and God said no: "My grace is sufficient for you, for my power is made perfect in weakness" (2 Corinthians 11:9). We should trust God that He always knows what's best for us, but we should also pray and believe He has the power to answer really big prayers!

What does Jesus tell His disciples they should do when they are praying in verse 25?

_____

_____

_____

Why does He say they should forgive that other person (v. 25)?

_____

_____

_____

Is there anyone in your life right now whom you need to forgive for something they have done to you? Write their name down.

_____

_____

We're going to spend some extra time praying today!

 PRAY: Pray now for God's help with the thing you're most worried about at the moment. Trust God that He has the power to act and that He knows your need even better than you do.

Think of a time you prayed and God answered your prayer in a really direct way. Praise Him for His kindness.

If you've ever felt really disappointed by God not answering your prayers for something you desperately wanted, bring that to Jesus now. Tell Him how you feel and ask Him for help to know whether you should keep praying that prayer or whether you just need to trust Him that He knows what's best, even when it makes no sense to us.

Ask God to help you forgive the person whose name you wrote down. Pray for God's blessing on them, and if they are not a Christian, pray that they would start following Jesus and have all their sins forgiven by God.

Pray that God would help you to grow in your trust in Him and in your prayerfulness.

THE JEWISH LEADERS
QUESTION JESUS' AUTHORITY

In the Disney film *Encanto*, the members of the Madrigal family each get a special power when they turn five. Pepa can control the weather. Isabela can make plants grow. Antonio can speak with animals. Dolores has superhuman hearing. Luisa has amazing strength. Bruno can see the future. As we've read through Mark's gospel so far, we've seen that Jesus doesn't have just one amazing power. He has them all. But where did He get His power and authority? That's what the chief priests want to know in today's passage.

Read Mark 11:27–33

When Jesus went back to the temple the day after He'd driven out the traders, what did the chief priests, teachers of the law, and elders ask Him (v. 28)?

Jesus offers them a deal in verse 29. What's His offer?

What question does Jesus ask the religious leaders back in verse 30?

FUN FACT: The religious leaders often try to trap Jesus. But here we see Jesus setting a trap for them instead.

In verses 31–32, the religious leaders think through the consequences of the two answers they could give to Jesus' question. What do they know He will say if they reply that John the Baptist's baptism came from heaven (v. 31)?

Why do they not want to reply that John the Baptist wasn't sent by God but that his baptism was just of human origin (v. 32)?

What did they finally say in answer to Jesus' question (v. 33)?

How does Jesus respond to their nonanswer (v. 33)?

FUN FACT: The temple was God's house, and throughout Mark's gospel, we've seen Jesus proving that He has God's own authority.

How did Jesus prove He had authority to forgive sins in Mark 2:10–12?

How did Jesus prove His authority over nature in Mark 4:39–41?

_____

_____

_____

How did Jesus prove His authority over death in Mark 5:41–42?

_____

_____

_____

How did Jesus prove His authority over sickness in Mark 11:51–52?

_____

_____

_____

What did Jesus say He was going to do with His authority in Mark 10:45?

_____

_____

_____

PRAY: Praise Jesus that He has authority to forgive sins, to heal the sick, to raise the dead, to calm storms, and to move mountains! Thank Jesus that He always uses His power for good and that He was willing to lay down His life for us.

JESUS TELLS A STORY AGAINST THE RELIGIOUS LEADERS

In our family, we sometimes play a game of trying to decide which character in a book or film each of us is like. For example, in the Harry Potter series, Miranda is like Hermione, and Eliza is like Ginny. In The Lord of the Rings, Rebecca secretly wants to be like the shieldmaiden Éowyn. (Oops, not so secret now!) In our passage today, Jesus tells a story, and when the religious leaders figure out who they are like in Jesus' story, they're not happy!

Read Mark 12:1–12

What did Jesus start to do in verse 1?

⇒FUN FACT: In Isaiah, God's people are compared to a vineyard, which God planted, but which did not produce good grapes, so God sent His judgment on the vineyard (Isaiah 5:1–7).

In Jesus' parable, what does the man do after he has planted the vineyard, put a wall around it, and built the winepress and the watch tower (v. 1)?

What did the man do at harvest time (v. 2)?

Instead of giving him some of the fruit, what did the tenants do with the vineyard owner's servant (v. 3)?

_____

_____

What did the owner do next (v. 4)?

_____

_____

What did the tenants do with the second servant (v. 4)?

_____

_____

What did the tenants do with the third servant the owner sent (v. 5)?

_____

_____

What kept happening every time the owner sent a servant (v. 5)?

_____

_____

Who did the owner send at last (v .6)?

_____

_____

Why did the owner send his son (v. 6)?

_____

_____

What did the tenants plan to do when the owner sent his son (v. 7)?

_____

_____

What did the tenants do with the owner's son (v. 8)?

_____

_____

What does Jesus say the owner will do (v. 9)?

_____

_____

✦FUN FACT: When Jesus enters Jerusalem on the colt, the shouting crowd echoes lines from Psalm 118:25–26. Now, Jesus quotes from just before those verses in Psalm 118:22–23: "The stone the builders rejected has become the cornerstone; the LORD has done this, and it is marvelous in our eyes."

How did the religious leaders react to Jesus' parable, and why (v. 12)?

_____

_____

_____

Who do you think the tenants represent in Jesus' parable?

_____

_____

Who do you think the owner represents?

_____

_____

Who do you think the son represents in Jesus' parable?

_____

_____

PRAY: Praise God the Father that He was willing to send His Son, whom He loves, to die for us. Thank Jesus that He loved us enough to come for us!

JESUS SHOWS GOD'S MORE IMPORTANT THAN CAESAR

In the United Kingdom, the pound coin has a picture of the Queen's head on it and shortened words in Latin meaning, "Elizabeth the second, by the grace of God, Queen." The coins used in Jesus' time and country had a picture of the Roman emperor, Tiberius. In our passage today, people are trying to trap Jesus again. But as usual, Jesus is much smarter than His enemies.

Read Mark 12:13–17

Looking back at verse 12, who sent some of the Pharisees and Herodians to try to trap Jesus (v. 13)?

_____

_____

✦FUN FACT: This is the second time in Mark that we've seen the Pharisees and the Herodians teaming up together. After Jesus healed a man with a shriveled hand on the Sabbath, "the Pharisees went out and began to plot with the Herodians how they might kill Jesus" (Mark 3:6). The Herodians were pro-Roman and the Pharisees were anti-Roman, so they made a weird team. But they agreed on hating Jesus.

What nice things do they say about Jesus in verse 14?

_____

_____

Do you think they really believed that Jesus taught "the way of God," or were they just trying to set Him up for a fall?

_____

_____

What question did they ask Jesus in verse 14?

What question does Jesus ask back to them (v. 15)?

According to verse 15, why does He ask them that question?

What does He tell them to do (v. 15)?

> ➡**FUN FACT:** The "imperial tax" they are talking about is probably a tax first required in AD 6 (when Jesus was a kid), and which started a revolt against the Romans led by a man named Judas the Galilean. The Jews who joined this rebellion believed that paying tax to the Romans showed that you were following the Roman emperor instead of God. The Romans crushed this rebellion. So now, if Jesus says that people *shouldn't* pay the tax, He could be arrested and crucified by the Romans. But if He says they *should* pay the tax, the Pharisees can claim that Jesus isn't really teaching the way of God.

➡**FUN FACT:** A denarius was a Roman coin worth about one day's wages for a laborer. It had a picture of the emperor Tiberius stamped on it and words in Latin that meant, "Tiberius Caesar, son of the divine Augustus." Caesar was a title that meant emperor. Tiberius' stepfather, Augustus, who was emperor before him, had been considered a god after he died, which is why the coins said "son of the divine Augustus."

What question does Jesus ask in verse 16?

How do the Pharisees and Herodians answer (v. 16)?

_____

_____

_____

How does Jesus finally respond to their question (v. 17)?

_____

_____

_____

➨**FUN FACT:** The first chapter of the Bible tells us that all human beings are made _in the image of God_ (Genesis 1:27). Just as the coins bore the image of the emperor, all human beings bear the image of God. God doesn't just own a portion of our money that we might pay in taxes or might give to care for the poor or to support missionary work. God owns us completely!

How did people respond to Jesus' answer (v. 17)?

_____

_____

_____

PRAY: Praise Jesus for how completely amazing He is! Ask God to help you recognize that you are made in His image and belong to Him completely. Pray for God's help to follow Jesus today.

JESUS SHOWS THAT GOD WILL RAISE THE DEAD

We've heard a lot about the Pharisees in Mark so far, but today, we're going to meet another religious group known as the Sadducees. The Sadducees had a lot of power over Jewish life. The high priests tended to be Sadducees, and most of the Jewish ruling council (the Sanhedrin) were Sadducees. In our passage today, they try to catch Jesus out just like the Pharisees did.

Read Mark 12:18–27

What does Mark tell us about the Sadducees in verse 18?

⇒✦FUN FACT: This Old Testament law comes from the book of Deuteronomy. It says, "If brothers are living together and one of them dies without a son, his widow must not marry outside the family. Her husband's brother shall take her and marry her and fulfill the duty of a brother-in-law to her. The first son she bears shall carry on the name of the dead brother so that his name will not be blotted out from Israel" (Deuteronomy 25:5–6). This law seems super weird to us in our culture! But it would have made a lot of sense in ancient Israel. It meant that the widow was taken care of, and that the dead man's name was carried on, which would have been seen as really important and honoring to him.

✦FUN FACT: The Pharisees believe that God's people would be raised to life again on judgment day. But the Sadducees did not believe in resurrection.

What Old Testament law do the Sadducees bring up in verse 19?

The Sadducees make up a situation to test Jesus. How many brothers were there in the story they present (v. 20)?

_____

_____

_____

How many of the brothers does the woman marry before she dies?

_____

_____

_____

What question do the Sadducees ask Jesus in verse 23?

_____

_____

_____

How sincere do you think the Sadducees were when they asked this?

_____

_____

_____

What two things does Jesus say the Sadducees don't know (v. 24)?

_____

_____

_____

What does Jesus say will not happen when God's people rise from the dead (v. 25)?

_____

_____

_____

What does Jesus say God's resurrected people will be like (v. 25)?

_____

_____

_____

_____

➔FUN FACT: This doesn't mean that we will be like the angels in every way. But just as the angels don't marry, so when God's people are raised from the dead on the last day, they will not marry. Marriage is only for this life, not for eternity, because it points us to the church's ultimate marriage to Jesus.

Jesus goes on to argue from a passage in the book of Exodus that death is not the end for God's people. What story does Jesus bring up (v. 26)?

_____

_____

_____

_____

➔FUN FACT: The Sadducees believed that only the first five books of the Bible (known as the Pentateuch) had authority from God. So, Jesus gives an example from one of these books when God speaks to Moses from a burning bush (Exodus 3:1–6).

How does God describe Himself in this story (v. 26)?

_____

_____

_____

_____

Abraham, Isaac, and Jacob had all died long before Moses was born. What point does Jesus make on the basis of this and God's statement (v. 27)?

_____

_____

_____

_____

PRAY: Praise God that He really will raise you to new life again one day, if you have put your trust in Jesus! Praise Him that this changes how we see everything on this earth, including marriage. Pray for help to believe the Scriptures and the power of God!

JESUS CALLS US TO LOVE GOD FIRST AND OTHERS AS OURSELVES

Do you have rules in your family? We don't have a list on the fridge, but we have plenty of rules. Some are more important than others. "Clear your plate after dinner" is less important than, "Don't hit your brother or sister." "Take your shoes off when you come in" is less important than, "Don't lie to your parents." There were many rules for God's people in the Old Testament law. But in our passage today, someone asks Jesus which one is most important.

Read Mark 12:28–34

What did this one teacher of the law notice about Jesus in verse 28?

_____

_____

What question did he ask Jesus (v. 29)?

_____

_____

✦FUN FACT: There are hundreds of laws in the Old Testament, so rabbis were often asked which were the most important. One famous example is a rabbi named Hillel, who is challenged by a Gentile to teach him the whole Jewish law while he (the Gentile) stands on one foot. Rabbi Hillel replies, "What is hateful to you, do not do to your neighbor; that is the entire Torah (i.e., law); the rest is commentary."[4]

What does Jesus say is the most important commandment (vv. 29–30)?

_____

_____

_____

➡✦FUN FACT: Jesus is quoting from Deuteronomy 6:4–5. This is the beginning of a group of memory verses that religious Jews would recite every morning and evening. Unlike the nations around them, the Jews believed in only *one* God, who created all things and who deserved their total worship.

What does Jesus say is the second most important commandment (v. 31)?

➡✦FUN FACT: Jesus quotes from Leviticus: "Do not seek revenge or bear a grudge against anyone among your people, but love your neighbor as yourself. I am the Lord" (Leviticus 19:18).

Most people in our culture today would agree that it is good to love other people as you love yourself. But Jesus puts this commandment second. Why do you think He does that?

If we love God more, do you think it will make us love other people more or less?

What does Jesus say about these two commandments together (v. 31)?

How does the teacher of the law respond in verse 32?

_____

_____

_____

What does he add in verse 33?

_____

_____

_____

➦**FUN FACT:** There are a lot of laws in the Old Testament about sacrifices and offerings that should be made in the temple. This is one of the ways in which God's people worshiped Him, and they point toward the day when Jesus comes as the real sacrifice: "The Lamb of God who takes away the sin of the world" (John 1:29). But the teacher of the law recognizes that Jesus is right to prioritize love for God and for others over any temple sacrifice.

What did Jesus say about this teacher of the law (v. 34)?

_____

_____

_____

What would this teacher of the law need to do to enter God's kingdom and not just be closer to it than the other teachers of the law?

_____

_____

_____

PRAY: Pray that God would help you love Him more and more: with all your heart and soul and mind and strength. Pray that He would help you love others like you love yourself. Thank Jesus that He came to be the real sacrifice and that His love for us does not depend on our goodness!

JESUS SHOWS THAT THE MESSIAH IS GREATER THAN KING DAVID

In our culture today, people tend to think that new things are better than old things and the present is better than the past. Sadly, elderly people in our culture are often treated like they're less important than young people, instead of having their wisdom respected. But in Jesus' day, people thought the opposite. Parents and grandparents and ancestors were given more honor than young people. A son would be less honored than a father. We need to understand this if we're going to get today's passage!

Read Mark 12:35–37

Where was Jesus in verse 35 and what was He doing?

What question does Jesus ask in verse 35?

Who does Jesus say inspired David as he spoke (v. 36)?

FUN FACT: The Holy Spirit of God inspired all the Bible authors as they wrote. Every word of the Bible is written by human beings, and every word is inspired by God. Jesus Himself makes this point about the Psalms, as He's about to quote one of the psalms that was written by King David.

➡FUN FACT: This is the beginning of Psalm 110. It's the Old Testament text most frequently quoted in the New Testament! If you turn to Psalm 110:1 in your Bible, you'll notice it says, "The LORD says to my Lord." You'll also notice that the first "LORD" is all in capital letters and you might wonder, "IS DAVID SHOUTING THAT WORD?" But the reason for the capital letters is that in the original Hebrew, David wrote the special name of God, which God gave to Moses when He spoke to him from a burning bush. Moses asked for God's name, and God said, "I AM WHO I AM!" (Exodus 3:14). Jews believed God's name was too sacred to be spoken aloud, so when they saw God's name in the text, they would say the Hebrew for "Lord." So, the first line of Psalm 110 means, "God said to my Lord."

What words of David does Jesus quote in verse 36?

What does God tell David's Lord to do (v. 36)?

Putting your enemies under your feet means to completely beat them! What question does Jesus then ask (v. 37)?

➡FUN FACT: As we've seen, in Jewish culture, a father would be seen as more worthy of honor than a son. Even once a son was grown up, the expectation would be that he would look up to his father, grandfather, great-grandfather, etc. But Jesus points out that the Messiah is called the "son of David," and yet David in Psalm 110 calls Him "my Lord." When Jesus asks how David's son can also be David's Lord, it's a bit like when He asked the rich man, "Why do you call me good? No one is good—except God alone" (Mark 10:18). He isn't saying that the Messiah *isn't* both the son of David and His Lord. He's pushing His audience to think about how shocking this is.

Psalm 110 talks about God's King defeating all His enemies. What do you think the Jews of Jesus' day were expecting the Messiah to defeat?

What has Jesus said He's planning to do instead (hint: Mark 10:33–34)?

_____

_____

_____

How is Jesus' death and resurrection a much greater victory than just throwing the Romans out of Israel would have been?

_____

_____

_____

How did the crowd react to Jesus' teaching (v. 37)?

_____

_____

_____

PRAY: Praise God that He sent Jesus to be the King who won by losing and who beat His enemies by dying for them. Praise Him that one day Jesus will come back to earth as universal Lord of all. Pray for someone you love who doesn't yet know Jesus, that he or she would see that Jesus is the rightful King before it's too late.

JESUS JUDGES POWERFUL TEACHERS AND PRAISES A POOR WIDOW

In today's passage, we see a sharp contrast between how Jesus speaks about two different kinds of people. First, Jesus criticizes the teachers of the law (which Miranda has started writing as TOTL!). Then, Jesus commends a poor widow. Most people of His day would have been much more impressed by the TOTL. But Jesus is much more impressed by the widow.

Read Mark 12:38–44

Who does Jesus warn people to watch out for in verse 38?

What examples does Jesus give of the TOTL showing off in verses 38–39?

People in our culture would show off in different ways than this. What examples of showing off in church might be similar to what the TOTL are doing here?

How is showing off like this the opposite of what Jesus taught about leadership in His kingdom (see Mark 10:42–44)?

What does Jesus accuse the TOTL of doing at the beginning of verse 40?

FUN FACT: Taking care of widows and orphans was a really important part of the Old Testament law. In Psalm 68:5, God is even called "a father to the fatherless, a defender of widows," because He cares about widows and orphans so much and calls His people to provide for them. But the teachers of the law of Jesus' day seem to be doing the opposite.

What else does Jesus accuse the TOTL of doing in verse 40?

Why do you think Jesus criticized the TOTL for showing off with long prayers to God while they were failing to take care of widows?

What does Jesus say will happen to the TOTL in the end (v. 40)?

Where did Jesus go and sit down in verse 41?

How much money were rich people putting in the temple treasury (v. 41)?

How much money did the poor widow put in (v. 42)?

What did Jesus say about the money the poor widow had put in compared to the money the rich people had put in (v. 43)?

How does Jesus explain what He means in verse 44?

✦FUN FACT: God doesn't need our money to do His work in the world. But He calls us to give today to support the spread of the gospel in the world and to care for the poor, so we can join in with His work.

Do you think the rich people felt good about how much money they were giving to God's work?

_____

_____

_____

How much faith did it take for the rich people to give a lot of money?

_____

_____

_____

How much faith did it take for the widow to put in her two small coins?

_____

_____

_____

PRAY: Ask God to help you be like the widow and unlike the teachers of the law. Pray that He would help you to be generous with even the small amount of money you have now and not to look for other people to praise you for the things you do at church, but instead to have a humble heart.

JESUS PREDICTS THE DESTRUCTION OF THE TEMPLE

On September 11, 2001, two planes were taken over by terrorists and flown into the two tallest buildings in New York City—the "Twin Towers" of the World Trade Center. No one was expecting this. The day before, it would have been impossible for people to imagine this happening. Thousands of people died in this terrible attack. In our passage today, Jesus warns His disciples that the most impressive building in their country is going to be destroyed. Unlike the Twin Towers, this building wasn't the business center of their country—it was the religious center.

Read Mark 13:1–13

⇒**SAD FACT:** The temple in Jerusalem was a massive and extremely impressive building. Jesus' claim that it was going to be destroyed would have been completely shocking news for His disciples. But it's exactly what happens in AD 70. The Romans retake Jerusalem after a Jewish rebellion against Roman rule, and they destroy the temple.

What does one of Jesus' disciples point out as they are leaving the temple (v. 1)?

What does Jesus say about the stones of the temple (v. 2)?

What do Peter, James, John, and Andrew ask Jesus privately (v. 4)?

What does Jesus warn them people will do in verse 5?

_____

_____

_____

➥**SERIOUS FACT:** Jesus teaches that one day He will come back to earth again as universal Lord of all. But, in this passage, He's warning His disciples not to believe people when they claim He's already come back again.

What does Jesus warn His disciples will happen in verse 8?

_____

_____

_____

What does Jesus tell His disciples will happen to them in verse 9?

_____

_____

_____

➥**SERIOUS FACT:** In the book of Acts, Jesus' disciples experience all the things that Jesus warns them about here.

What does Jesus say must happen (v. 10)?

_____

_____

_____

What does Jesus say His disciples shouldn't worry about when they are arrested and brought to trial (v. 11)?

_____

_____

_____

What reason does Jesus give for why His disciples shouldn't worry about what they will say (v. 11)?

_____

_____

_____

What does Jesus say will happen in people's families (v. 12)?

_____

_____

_____

How does Jesus say people will feel about His disciples because of Him (v. 13)?

_____

_____

What does Jesus say will happen to anyone who stands firm, despite being hated (v. 13)?

_____

_____

How does the warning and promise in verse 13 encourage you as you stand for Jesus in front of friends or family members who disagree with your beliefs?

_____

_____

_____

PRAY: Pray for the Lord's help as you stand for your faith in Jesus at school or in your neighborhood. Pray for other Christians around the world today who face imprisonment and beatings for being Christians, just like Jesus' first disciples did. Thank God that He has sent His Holy Spirit to help us even today as we share our faith in Jesus with others who might hate us for it.

JESUS WARNS ABOUT THE END OF THE WORLD

The dad in our family (Bryan) loves climbing. He has a dream of going to Mount Everest—not to climb it, just to look at it. The problem is, you can't see the summit of Mount Everest from base camp because other massive mountains block your view. Sometimes, people compare prophecies in the Bible to looking at a mountain range. Often, there would be a short-term fulfillment of the prophecy people could see from where they were, but also a long-term fulfillment that might be hundreds or thousands of years away. In today's passage, Jesus talks about some events that would happen soon. Some we are still waiting for almost two thousand years later.

Read Mark 13:14–27

When does Jesus say that people in Judea should flee to the mountains (v. 14)?

What does Jesus tell people not to do when that time comes (vv. 15–16)?

⇒ **SERIOUS FACT**: The "abomination that causes desolation" was first mentioned in the book of Daniel. Daniel was living in exile in Babylon after the first temple was destroyed. An angel told him that one day the temple would be rebuilt and the Anointed One would come. But afterward, the Anointed One would be put to death and Jerusalem and the sanctuary would be destroyed by an enemy ruler, who would set up "an abomination that causes desolation" at the temple (Daniel 9:25–27). When Jesus spoke these words, the first part of this prophecy had already happened: the temple had been rebuilt and the Anointed One (Jesus) had come. But He had not yet been put to death, and the temple had not been destroyed again. Experts disagree about what exactly Jesus meant by the "abomination that causes desolation."

Who does Jesus say it will be extra hard for when that time comes (v. 17)?

_____

_____

How bad does Jesus say things will be when that time comes (v. 19)?

_____

_____

_____

Why does Jesus say the Lord has cut that time short (v. 20)?

_____

_____

_____

How does Jesus say His disciples should respond to people who say they've found the Messiah in the future (vv. 21–23)?

_____

_____

_____

➦**SERIOUS FACT:** Experts disagree about whether Jesus is describing what will happen to Jerusalem in AD 70 throughout this speech or whether He is talking at least some of the time about the last day when He will come back again to rule. The Roman attack on Jerusalem in AD 70 was really, really terrible. But some of what Jesus says in verses 24–27 seems to fit better with what will happen when He comes back again.

What does Jesus say will happen to the sun, moon, and stars (vv. 24–25)?

_____

_____

_____

Who does Jesus say will come in clouds with power and glory (v. 26)?

_____

_____

What will Jesus send His angels to do at that time (v. 27)?

_____

_____

_____

➨**FUN FACT:** "From the four winds, from the ends of the earth to the ends of the heavens" means all over the world. Today, Jesus' followers live all across the world, just like He said they would!

What does Jesus say will not pass away until all these things have happened (v. 30)?

_____

_____

_____

What does Jesus say will pass away in the end, and what won't (v. 31)?

_____

_____

_____

➨**FUN FACT:** Some people think the generation Jesus is talking about is the literal lifespan of His hearers, many of whom will live to see the temple in Jerusalem destroyed. Others think "this generation" means this age, between when Jesus first came and when He will come again as Lord of all.

PRAY: Praise Jesus that He is the rightful King of all the universe and that one day we will see Him coming on the clouds with great power and glory. Pray that more and more people would put their trust in Jesus now.

JESUS TELLS HIS DISCIPLES TO GET READY!

Imagine your teacher assigned your class a test and then left the room while you worked on it. If she said she'd be gone for half an hour, I bet everyone would get the test done right away. But if she said she'd be gone for an hour, some people would do the test and some people would mess around with their friends and have fun before they started. What if you didn't know when the teacher would be back? Jesus taught that no one knows when He's going to come back, so we need to be ready any time!

Read Mark 13:28–37

Who knows the day and hour when Jesus will come back (v. 32)?

_____

_____

_____

How does Jesus say we should act, since we don't know when that day will come (v. 33)?

_____

_____

_____

✦FUN FACT: In Mark 12:1–12, Jesus tells a story in which He compares God to a vineyard owner who rents His vineyard out to tenants and goes away. In today's passage, He compares Himself to a man going away and leaving his servants in charge of his house.

What does Jesus tell the servant at the door to do (v. 34)?

What does Jesus tell His disciples to do in verse 35?

Why does He say they should keep watch (v. 35)?

What are the three times of day that Jesus gives as examples of when the owner might come back (v. 35)?

What might the servants be doing at those times if they aren't keeping watch?

What does Jesus say His disciples shouldn't let Him find them doing when He comes back (v. 36)?

Do you think this means that Christians should never go to sleep?

What do you think it does mean for us to be ready for Jesus to return?

→**VITAL FACT:** The most important way you can be ready for Jesus' return is by saying sorry to God for your sin and putting your trust in Jesus. His death on the cross pays for all our sin, if we will only turn to Him. And when we do, we are covered in Jesus' goodness in God's eyes. It's like we've taken off our dirty clothes and put on Jesus' clean clothes instead! If you haven't put your trust in Jesus yet, do it today!

If you are trusting in Jesus, that means you're one of His servants on this earth, and He's given all of His servants work to do. Here's a check-list of the kinds of things we should be doing while we wait:

☐ Telling other people the good news about Jesus and praying that they would repent and believe in Him

☐ Caring for people who don't have enough money by sharing some of ours

☐ Welcoming people who are lonely or left out

☐ Helping people who are sick or suffering

☐ Protecting people who are getting hurt by others

☐ Loving our enemies

☐ Forgiving those who hurt us

The list could go on! But we should make sure we are doing things we would not be ashamed to be caught doing if Jesus came back today . . . because He might!

 PRAY: Pray that God would help you be ready for when Jesus returns. Thank Him that Jesus' death in our place washes away all our sin and all the ways we fail to live as His servants should. Pray that God would help you serve Jesus throughout the whole of your life, so that you're ready whenever He comes or whenever He calls you back to Him at the end of your life.

Well done! You've made it to the end of Act 5!

JESUS TAKES GOD'S JUDGMENT AND BEATS DEATH!

This final act of Mark's story begins with a woman anointing Jesus for His burial and ends with three women going to anoint Jesus' buried body and finding that He's risen from the dead!

In Act 6, we'll see Jesus betrayed by Judas and denied by Peter, who had sworn that he'd die with Jesus if he needed to. We'll see Him calling broken bread His body and calling a cup of wine a new covenant in His blood. We'll see Him praying to His Father that He *wouldn't* have to drink the cup of God's wrath against our sin, but doing it anyway. We'll see Jesus being condemned by the Jewish leaders, handed over to the Roman governor, mockingly crowned by Roman soldiers, crucified for claiming to be the King of the Jews, and refusing to save Himself—so He could save us.

We'll see Him calling out to God in agony on the cross and breathing His last breath, and then we'll see the curtain in the temple being torn in two from top to bottom, as Jesus opens up to the way back to God's presence by His death.

Finally, we'll see Him buried by a man named Joseph, while two women named Mary watch. And we'll see those women coming back on the third day and finding that He's been raised back to life!

Act 1: Mark 1–2 **JESUS IS GOD'S PROMISED KING**	Act 6: Mark 14–16 **JESUS TAKES GOD'S JUDGMENT AND BEATS DEATH**
Act 2: Mark 3–5 **JESUS STARTS HIS KINGDOM FAMILY**	Act 5: Mark 11–13 **JESUS ENTERS JERUSALEM AS KING**
Act 3: Mark 6–8:26 **JESUS GROWS HIS KINGDOM FAMILY**	Act 4: Mark 8:27–10:52 **JESUS TURNS GOD'S KINGDOM UPSIDE DOWN**

JESUS IS ANOINTED
FOR HIS BURIAL

What's the best gift you've ever received? Maybe it was a birthday present or a Christmas present and it was just exactly what you'd asked for—or perhaps it was a total surprise, and someone who loved you knew you well enough to guess what you would want. In our story today, Jesus receives a really special gift from someone who loved Him very much. Others complained it was a waste. But Jesus disagreed.

Read Mark 14:1–11

In verse 1, what special holidays does Mark tell us were coming up in two days?

‚àö**FUN FACT:** The Passover was a yearly celebration of when God rescued His people out of Egypt. God told each family to sacrifice a lamb and smear some of its blood over their door so that when the Angel of Death went through the land, their home would be protected. The Feast of Unleavened Bread continued for the week after the Passover. Lots of Jews came to Jerusalem for Passover.

What were the chief priests and TOTL plotting (v. 1)?

Why did they not want to kill Jesus during the Passover festival (v. 2)?

Bethany was a village near Jerusalem, where Jesus often stayed when He visited Jerusalem. At whose house was Jesus having dinner in verse 3?

What did the woman who came into the house do (v. 3)?

➥**FUN FACT:** John tells us who this woman was. Her name was Mary. We hear more about Mary and her sister Martha in Luke 11:38–42, and in John 11, when Jesus raises their brother, Lazarus, from the dead! Jesus really loved Mary (John 11:5). And she really loved Him back!

What did some of the people watching say (v. 4)?

What did they say should have been done with the perfume instead (v. 5)?

➥**FUN FACT:** In John's gospel, Judas Iscariot is identified as the one who criticized Mary for her actions—not because he cared about the poor, but because he liked to steal money from the money bag (John 12:6).

How did Jesus respond to the people who were rebuking Mary harshly (v. 6)?

We know from earlier in Mark that Jesus really cared about the poor. How does he respond to the claim that the money should have been given to the poor (v. 7)?

_____

_____

_____

What does Jesus say that Mary has done to His body (v. 8)?

_____

_____

✦**FUN FACT:** In Jesus' day, people prepare a dead body for burial by anointing it with various things that will preserve the body and make it smell good. Jesus says that Mary has got this process started with His body—which is soon to die and be buried. This isn't what Mary would have planned, but it's how Jesus received her gift.

What amazing statement does Jesus make about Mary's action in verse 9?

_____

_____

What does Judas Iscariot do right afterward (v. 10)?

_____

_____

_____

How did the chief priests react to Judas's offer to betray Jesus (v. 11)?

_____

_____

_____

PRAY: Pray that God would make you more like Mary: willing to "waste" whatever is most valuable to you on Jesus. Praise God that Jesus' promise that her action would be remembered has come true!

JESUS PREDICTS
JUDAS'S BETRAYAL

Have you ever been really let down by a close friend? Maybe you'd spent a lot of time together. He or she had been to your house tons of times. You'd told them your secrets and really trusted them. Then one day they just stopped being your friend—or worse, started saying nasty things about you to other people. It really hurts when someone does that. Yesterday, we saw Judas Iscariot going to betray Jesus to His enemies. Today, we'll see that Jesus knew what Judas was up to.

Read Mark 14:12–21

What day was it in verse 12?

_____

_____

What did the disciples ask Jesus (v. 12)?

_____

_____

What does Jesus tell two of His disciples to do (v. 13)?

_____

_____

_____

What does Jesus tell His disciples to say to the owner of the house (v. 14)?

_____

_____

_____

What does Jesus say the owner will show the disciples (v. 15)?

_____

_____

_____

What do Jesus' disciples find when they follow His instructions (v. 16)?

_____

_____

_____

➡️**FUN FACT:** Just like when Jesus sent His disciples to get a colt for Him to ride into Jerusalem (Mark 11:1–6), He's totally in control of this situation.

What does Jesus say when He was eating with His disciples that evening (v. 17)?

_____

_____

_____

How did Jesus' disciples feel when He said this (v. 19)?

_____

_____

_____

What did they each say (v. 19)?

_____

_____

_____

How does Jesus respond (v. 20)?

_____

_____

What does Jesus say about Himself in verse 20?

What does Jesus say about the person who betrays Him (v. 21)?

How does this conversation show us once again that Jesus is completely in control as He heads toward His death?

See if you can remember our memory verse from Mark 10:45. Try to write it down. If you can't remember all of it, look it up and write it down and have another practice. We're getting close to the part of Mark's gospel where Jesus gives His life, just like He planned.

 PRAY: Praise Jesus that He was not just a passive victim of His circumstances, but that He knew exactly what was going to happen, even down to which of His disciples would betray Him. Tell God about a time when you felt deeply hurt by a friend letting you down, and thank Him that Jesus knows exactly how this feels. Pray that God would help you to be a faithful friend and a faithful follower of Jesus.

JESUS SHOWS THAT HE'S THE SACRIFICE

At the beginning of the 2005 film *Nanny McPhee*, Mr. Brown's seven children have come up with yet another plan for scaring their latest nanny away. The nanny runs to the funeral home where Mr. Brown works screaming, "They've eaten the baby!" Of course, the children haven't really done this. But they've hidden the baby in a large pot, and they're eating chicken legs to prank the nanny. In today's passage, Jesus makes a claim to His disciples that would have shocked them about as much as the nanny was shocked. Except that He's not joking.

Read Mark 14:22–26

What did Jesus take and break while His disciples were eating (v. 22)?

_____

_____

_____

What did Jesus say to His disciples about the bread He'd just torn up (v. 22)?

_____

_____

_____

How do you think the disciples would have felt when Jesus did this?

_____

_____

_____

⇒✦FUN FACT: It was normal for the host of a Passover meal to take bread, bless it, break it, and pass it out. But what Jesus says about the bread here would have been shocking! Not only was He saying that His body would be all torn up, He was also inviting His disciples to eat His body, pictured in the bread.

What did Jesus do with the cup of wine in verse 23?

What did Jesus say the wine they were drinking was in verse 24?

What did Jesus say about His covenant blood in verse 24?

⇒✦FUN FACT: A covenant is a binding promise or agreement. For example, God makes a covenant with Abraham when He promises to make his descendants as many as the stars (Genesis 15:18). Covenants were often confirmed with a sacrifice. For example, after the Israelites agree to the law God had given them, Moses takes the blood of sacrificed bulls and sprinkles it on the people, saying, "This is the blood of the covenant that the LORD has made with you in accordance with all these words" (Exodus 24:8). But Jesus is making a new covenant in His *own* blood.

⇒✦FUN FACT: The idea of blood being "poured out" would have made Jesus' disciples think of animal sacrifices in God's temple. Jesus says that His blood of the covenant is poured out "for many." Matthew's gospel adds, "for the forgiveness of sins" (Matthew 26:28).

How does Jesus' claim that His blood is poured out "for many" remind you of our memory verse in Mark 10:45?

When does Jesus say He will drink wine again (v. 25)?

_____

_____

_____

FUN FACT: Jesus is God's King, and one day He will come back in power and glory to take up His kingdom over all the world. This meal with His disciples prepares them for His death and also points them forward to when He comes again. The apostle Paul explains it like this:

> The Lord Jesus, on the night he was betrayed, took bread, and when he had given thanks, he broke it and said, "This is my body, which is for you; do this in remembrance of me." In the same way, after supper he took the cup, saying, "This cup is the new covenant in my blood; do this, whenever you drink it, in remembrance of me." For whenever you eat this bread and drink this cup, you proclaim the Lord's death until he comes. (1 Corinthians 11:23–26)

This is why most churches celebrate the "Lord's Supper" either every week or every month as a reminder of Jesus' death for us.

PRAY: Praise God that Jesus' body was broken for you and His blood was poured out for you! Pray that you would always be amazed by this and that you would look forward to when Jesus comes again!

JESUS PREDICTS
PETER'S DENIAL

At the end of the first book in The Lord of the Rings, Boromir—a member of the fellowship assembled to help Frodo destroy the ring—tries to take the ring for himself. After seeing a friend turn on him like this, Frodo decides that he needs to go on to Mordor alone. But when his best friend, Sam, realizes that Frodo has left, he tracks him down and insists on going with him. Frodo complains that he'd be safely on his way if Sam hadn't come. "Safely!" said Sam. "All alone and without me to help you? I couldn't have borne it, it'd have been the death of me." "It would be the death of you to come with me, Sam," said Frodo. "And I could not have borne that."[5] In our passage today, Peter sees himself as being like Sam: ready to go with his master even to death. But Jesus says he's not.

Read Mark 14:27–31

➡IMPORTANT FACT:
Jesus is quoting from the prophet Zechariah, where God says,"Awake, sword, against my shepherd, against the man who is close to me . . . Strike the shepherd, and the sheep will be scattered" (Zechariah 13:7). In Zechariah, shepherds represent kings. Jesus is making a connection: He is God's ultimate King who will be struck down by God Himself, while His sheep are scattered.

What does Jesus say about His disciples in verse 27?

How does Jesus explain why He thinks this (v. 27)?

What promise does Jesus make to His disciples in verse 28?

_____

_____

_____

What does this show about how Jesus will treat His disciples after they have let Him down?

_____

_____

_____

➦**SERIOUS FACT:** Jesus has predicted His death and resurrection multiple times so far in Mark. When He first told His disciples He was going to be killed and then would rise again, Peter tried to talk Him out of it (Mark 8:32). Now, Peter speaks up again.

How does Peter respond to Jesus saying that all His disciples will fall away (v. 29)?

_____

_____

_____

What can we learn from this about how Peter sees himself, compared with the other disciples?

_____

_____

_____

What does Jesus say to Peter (v. 30)?

_____

_____

_____

➡✦FUN FACT: In Jesus' day, people didn't have watches or phones with clocks on them, so they had other ways of marking time. The rooster crowing was a sign that the night had ended and the day had begun. Jesus is emphasizing here that Peter will disown Him—say he has nothing to do with Jesus—three times before the night is over.

What did Peter claim in response (v. 31)?

What did all the other disciples say (v. 31)?

What do you think you would have said if you had been one of Jesus' disciples that night?

How does their attitude show that they trust themselves more than they trust Jesus' words?

PRAY: Praise Jesus that He was ready to go to the cross alone. Ask God to help you trust Jesus more than you trust yourself. Praise Him that He knows all your sin and weakness and still loves you more than you could ever imagine!

JESUS PRAYS FOR A CUP TO BE TAKEN AWAY

Have you ever wondered how Jesus felt about going to the cross? He's the greatest hero that the world has ever seen, so we might think that it was no big deal. After all, Jesus could stop storms and raise the dead just with His words! But in our passage today, we see that Jesus deeply dreaded the cross. This wasn't just because it was an incredibly painful way to die. It was because He knew that on the cross, He'd take God's judgment for our sin.

Read Mark 14:32–42

Where did Jesus and His disciples go (v. 32)?

✦FUN FACT: Gethsemane was probably a privately owned olive grove on the Mount of Olives. You could look across from there to the hill on which the temple was built.

What did Jesus tell His disciples to do (v. 32)?

Who did Jesus take with Him (v. 33)?

✦FUN FACT: This is the same small group of disciples who witnessed Jesus' transfiguration (Mark 9:2). They seem to be His inner circle. But all three of them have already made big mistakes (see Mark 8:31–33 and 10:35–40).

What did Jesus tell Peter, James, and John about how He felt in verse 34?

What did He tell them to do (v. 34)?

What did Jesus do with His body in verse 35?

What two names did Jesus use for God in verse 36?

➔FUN FACT: *Abba* is an Aramaic word. Mark is written in Greek, but at special moments, Mark keeps words in Aramaic, which was Jesus' first language.

What does Jesus ask His Father to do (v. 36)?

Whose will does Jesus say He'll follow in verse 36?

What are Peter, James, and John doing when Jesus comes back (v. 37)?

What does Jesus tell them to do instead (v. 38)?

When Jesus went to pray again and then came back, what were they doing (v. 40)?

When Jesus went to pray a third time and then came back, what were they doing (v. 41)?

What does Jesus say is happening to Him (the Son of Man) in verse 41?

What does this show about the answer the Father gave to Jesus' prayer?

PRAY: Thank Jesus for going to the cross, despite how unbearable He knew that it would be. Praise Him that He was willing to take our sin on His shoulders and bear the punishment for all of us.

JUDAS BETRAYS JESUS

When Harry Potter was a baby, his parents were murdered by Voldemort. They'd known that Voldemort was after them. But they were under a protective spell, which meant he couldn't find them. The spell required a friend of theirs to be the "secret keeper." As long as their friend didn't tell anyone where Lily and James Potter were hiding, they were safe. But their secret keeper friend betrayed them. Today, we see one of Jesus' disciples do the same to Him.

Read Mark 14:43–52

What had Jesus just said (v. 42)?

_____

_____

Who showed up while He was still speaking (v. 43)?

_____

_____

Who came along with Judas, and what were they armed with (v. 43)?

_____

_____

_____

Who had sent this armed crowd (v. 43)?

_____

_____

↠✦FUN FACT: When Jesus first predicts His death, He says that He will be rejected by "the elders, the chief priests and the teachers of the law" (Mark 8:31). These three groups are the very people who order Jesus' arrest.

What had Judas told the armed crowd he would do to identify Jesus (v. 44)?

_____

_____

What had Judas told the armed crowd to do after he'd kissed Jesus (v. 44)?

_____

_____

What did Judas do to Jesus, and what did he say (v. 45)?

_____

_____

↠✦FUN FACT: Jesus also predicts that one of His chosen twelve disciples will betray Him, and here we see Judas doing exactly what Jesus said would happen. Earlier that night, Judas would have been with the other disciples when they all said they would rather die with Him than disown Him (Mark 14:31). But now Judas is betraying his rabbi with a kiss.

What did the armed men do to Jesus as soon as Judas had kissed Him (v. 46)?

_____

_____

_____

What did one of Jesus' disciples do in response (v. 47)?

_____

_____

_____

↠✦FUN FACT: In John's gospel we find out that it is Peter who cuts off the ear of the high priest's servant, and that the servant's name is Malchus (John 18:10). In Luke's gospel, we find that Jesus touches Malchus's ear and heals him (Luke 22:51).

What did Jesus ask the armed crowd (v. 48)?

What does Jesus point out He's been doing (v. 49)?

Why does Jesus say His arrest is happening this way (v. 49)?

What do all His disciples do at this point (v. 50)?

How is this different from what they had all said that they would do in verse 31?

What happened to one young man who had been following Him (v. 51)?

How brave were Jesus' disciples when the moment came for courage?

PRAY: Praise Jesus that He was brave for us when we would all have run away like the disciples. Pray that He would help you to be brave in standing for your faith in Him today. Thank Him for His kindness and forgiveness.

JESUS IS CONDEMNED
BY THE RELIGIOUS LEADERS

When Peter first recognized that Jesus really was the Messiah, Jesus predicted He would be rejected by the elders, the chief priests, and the TOTL (Mark 8:31). In our passage today, we see that happening.

Read Mark 14:53–65

Who was Jesus taken to in verse 53, and who else was there (vv. 53–54)?

_____

_____

_____

Who followed Jesus at a distance, and what did he do (v. 54)?

_____

_____

➥FUN FACT: The Sanhedrin was the Jewish ruling council or high court. It consisted of seventy-one men and was led by the high priest. The Romans gave the Sanhedrin limited authority to judge, but not to sentence anyone to death. They could only make that recommendation to the Roman authorities.

What were the chief priests and the Sanhedrin looking for (v. 55)?

_____

_____

_____

Did they find any evidence that would justify putting Jesus to death (v. 55)?

_____

_____

What was the problem with the false testimony against Jesus (v. 56)?

What false testimony did some people come up with in verse 58?

✦**FUN FACT:** In John's gospel, when Jesus is asked to prove His authority, He replies, "Destroy this temple, and I will raise it again in three days." John clarifies that the temple Jesus was speaking of was His body (John 2:19–21). And Jesus' accusers in Mark claim that Jesus said *He* would destroy the temple, which isn't what Jesus said.

What did the high priest ask Jesus (v. 60)?

What answer did Jesus give (v. 61)?

What did the high priest ask Jesus next (v. 61)?

How does Jesus respond to the high priest's question (v. 62)?

✦**FUN FACT:** As we saw on Day 48, when Moses asks God for His name, God replies, "I AM WHO I AM" (Exodus 3:14). In John's gospel, Jesus makes multiple "I AM" statements—for example, "Before Abraham was born, I am!" (John 8:58). This is one way Jesus claims to be God. Here in Mark, when Jesus answers the high priest's question as to whether He is the Messiah, Jesus responds, "I am!"

Read Mark 13:26. How is what Jesus said to His disciples similar to what He says to the high priest now (v. 62)?

_____

_____

_____

What does the high priest do when he hears Jesus say this (v. 63)?

_____

_____

_____

Why does the high priest think Jesus is blaspheming (i.e., insulting) God?

_____

_____

_____

What does the Sanhedrin agree (v. 64)?

_____

_____

_____

What do some of them do to Jesus (v. 65)?

_____

_____

_____

 PRAY: Thank God that Jesus was willing to face an unjust trial and that He understands when people say things about us that aren't true. Pray that God would help you believe that Jesus really is God's King, who will one day come again on the clouds of heaven!

PETER DENIES
JESUS

Think of the most shameful thing you've ever done. Maybe you told a terrible lie. Maybe you were really mean to a younger kid. Perhaps you stole something and never gave it back. Maybe someone trusted you with a secret and you told someone else to make fun of them. Now, imagine you had a choice: you could tell everyone you know about that awful thing you did, or you could keep it a secret. Which would you choose? In today's passage, we see Peter's most shameful moment and we find out what he chose.

Read Mark 14:66–72

Where was Peter (v. 66)?

_____

_____

_____

Who came up to Peter while he was in the courtyard (v. 66)?

_____

_____

_____

What did the servant girl do (v. 67)?

_____

_____

_____

What did she say to Peter (v. 67)?

⇒✦FUN FACT: In Jesus' day, people didn't have last names. Jesus (which is the same name as Joshua) was a common name, so Jesus is often referred to as "Jesus of Nazareth" to distinguish Him from others with that name. The high priest's servant girl calls Him "that Nazarene, Jesus."

What did Peter say in response to the servant girl's claim (v. 68)?

What did the servant girl say when she saw Peter in the entryway (v. 69)?

How did Peter react (v. 70)?

What happened a bit later (v. 71)?

⇒✦FUN FACT: Nazareth, where Jesus was raised, was in a northern region known as Galilee, and it seems that Galileans had a different accent from people who came from Judea in the south where Jerusalem was and where this scene takes place. In Matthew's gospel, the bystanders add, "Your accent gives you away" (Matthew 26:73).

How does Peter respond to this third claim that he's a follower of Jesus (v. 71)?

What happens as soon as Peter swears he doesn't even know Jesus (v. 72)?

What does Peter remember when he hears the rooster (v. 72)?

What does Peter do when he remembers Jesus' words (v. 72)?

✦**FUN FACT:** As we learned in the introduction to this study, Mark's gospel is likely based on Peter's memories. Peter could probably have chosen to keep this story secret. After all, many things that happened during Jesus' ministry get left out of the Gospels because there wasn't room for them. But all four gospels tell this story of Peter denying Jesus, just like Jesus said he would.

Peter went on to be one of the key leaders of the early church. What do we learn about Jesus from the fact that He still let Peter lead after this?

How does Peter's story encourage us today when we mess up big time?

PRAY: Praise Jesus that He is the only real hero in the Bible. Thank Him that He doesn't reject us, even when we fail like Peter, but that He uses losers like us to witness to His gospel. Pray that He would give you a repentant heart, like Peter's, to recognize when you've messed up and to be deeply sorry.

JESUS IS SENT TO BE CRUCIFIED WHILE A CRIMINAL GOES FREE

If you could trade places with anyone, who would you pick? Perhaps a singer or a sports star. Or maybe someone super rich or beautiful or smart? Today, we see someone trading places with Jesus. That person had been condemned to death, but he went free, while Jesus headed to the cross.

Read Mark 15:1–15

What did the chief priests, elders, and teachers of the law do to Jesus (v. 1)?

➥FUN FACT: Pontius Pilate was the Roman governor of Judea from AD 26 to 36. The Roman historian Tacitus (who didn't like Christians at all) confirms that Jesus was executed under the authority of this governor.

What question did Pilate ask Jesus (v. 2)?

How did Jesus answer (v. 2)?

What did Jesus say in response to all the accusations against Him (v. 5)?

_____

_____

_____

What custom does Mark tell us about in verse 6?

_____

_____

_____

What does Mark tell us about the prisoner named Barabbas (v. 7)?

_____

_____

_____

➔**FUN FACT:** An insurrection means a violent rebellion against a government.

Who did Pilate offer to release to the crowd when they came to claim a prisoner, according to the custom (v. 9)?

_____

_____

_____

Why did Pilate offer to release Jesus (v. 10)?

_____

_____

_____

Who did the chief priests persuade the crowd to ask for instead (v. 11)?

_____

_____

➡✦FUN FACT: As we saw when Jesus was praying in Gethsemane, *abba* is the Aramaic word for "father," so Barabbas means "son of the father." Abba was a common name, so it was probably just this guy's dad's name. But it's interesting that he went free, while Jesus—the Son of the heavenly Father—did not.

What did Pilate ask the crowd in verse 12?

_____

_____

How did they respond (v. 13)?

_____

_____

What does Pilate ask the crowd in verse 14?

_____

_____

How did they respond (v. 14)?

_____

_____

What did Pilate do to Barabbas to make the crowd happy (v. 15)?

_____

_____

Remember our memory verse: Mark 10:45? In today's passage, Jesus—who is innocent—takes the place of Barabbas—who is guilty. This is a little picture of the ransom Jesus paid for us. He gave His life so we could live. He took God's punishment for our sin so that we could go free!

 PRAY: Praise the Father for sending Jesus to take our place. Thank Jesus that He was willing to pay the price for our sin. Pray that more and more people would accept His offer of forgiveness and new life!

THE ROMAN SOLDIERS
MOCK KING JESUS

Have you ever been bullied? I hope not. It's a terrible experience. Bullying can be physical or emotional. Both kinds are deeply painful. In our passage today, Jesus experiences physical and emotional bullying. Jesus had just been flogged, and now the Roman soldiers have fun by beating Him up some more and laughing at Him.

Read Mark 15:16–20

Where did the soldiers take Jesus in verse 16?

✦FUN FACT: The Praetorium was the courtyard of Pilate's headquarters.

Who did the soldiers in charge of Jesus call (v. 16)?

Why do you think they called the whole company of soldiers?

What did the soldiers put on Jesus' body (v. 17)?

What did they put on Jesus' head (v. 17)?

_____

_____

FUN FACT: A king or ruler would have worn a purple robe and a conquering hero or victorious athlete would have worn a laurel wreath on his head. So, the soldiers are dressing Jesus up to look like a fake version of a king or hero.

What did the soldier call out to Jesus (v. 18)?

_____

_____

_____

What did they do to His head (v. 19)?

_____

_____

_____

What else did they do to Him (v. 19)?

_____

_____

_____

FUN FACT: Paying homage to someone means showing reverence or respect, especially to a king. The Greek word Mark uses here can also mean to worship. So, the soldiers are totally mocking the idea that Jesus is the King of the Jews.

What did the soldiers do when they had finished mocking Him (v. 20)?

_____

_____

_____

➡️***IMPORTANT FACT:*** Jesus has predicted everything that is going to happen to Him, including this bullying by the Roman soldiers. The third time He predicts His death to His disciples, He says, "The Son of Man will be delivered over to the chief priests and teachers of the law. They will condemn him to death and will hand him over to the Gentiles, who will mock him and spit on him, flog him and kill him" (Mark 10:33–34).

Many of the Jews were hoping that the Messiah would beat the Romans and throw them out of Jerusalem. How is Jesus' plan the opposite of this?

So far in Mark's gospel, we've seen Jesus showing His power to calm storms, heal sickness, multiply food, and walk on water. Do you think He could have stood up to the soldiers if He'd chosen to?

Why do you think Jesus let the soldiers treat Him like this?

How can this story help us when we're being mocked for following Him?

PRAY: Praise Jesus that He was willing to be mocked and beaten up, even though He really is the King—not only of the Jews, but of the whole universe. Pray that He would help you in times when you face mockery for following Him.

JESUS IS CRUCIFIED
TO SAVE OTHERS

Crucifixion was the most horrible way to die. The Romans used it as a punishment for people who rebelled against their rule, so that anyone else who was thinking of rebelling would see how awful it was and change their mind. It was extremely painful and long-lasting, and crucifixions happened in public so that everyone could see. In today's passage, we see Jesus crucified.

Read Mark 15:21–32

Who was passing by on his way into Jerusalem from the countryside (v. 21)?

What did the Roman soldiers make him do (v. 21)?

⇥FUN FACT: Experts think Mark mentions Simon of Cyrene's sons, Rufus and Alexander, because they later became Christians and told their father's story.

Where did the Roman soldiers take Jesus (v. 22)?

What did they offer Jesus to drink (v. 23)?

Did Jesus take the drink (v. 23)?

_____

_____

➡️**SAD FACT:** This offer of wine mixed with myrrh might be part of the soldiers' mockery of Jesus, or it might be meant to dull the pain a bit.

What did they do to Jesus (v. 24)?

_____

_____

What did they do with His clothes (v. 24)?

_____

_____

➡️**FUN FACT:** Casting lots was like throwing dice. Psalm 22 describes many of the things that happened to Jesus when He is crucified, including: "They divide my clothes among them and cast lots for my garments" (Psalm 22:18).

What did the charge against Jesus say (v. 26)?

_____

_____

Who was crucified along with Jesus (v. 27)?

_____

_____

What did those passing by Jesus as He was crucified say (vv. 29–30)?

_____

_____

_____

Could Jesus have come down from the cross if He had chosen to?

_____

_____

How did the chief priests and teachers of the law mock Jesus in verse 31?

_____

_____

_____

➡**IMPORTANT FACT:** Jesus saves others by *not* saving Himself. He was dying in our place so we could live, giving His own life as a ransom for us.

What do the religious leaders say Jesus should do if He's really the Messiah (v. 32)?

_____

_____

What do they say that they would do if He came down from the cross (v. 32)?

_____

_____

What did the rebels crucified on either side of Jesus do (v. 32)?

_____

_____

➡**AMAZING FACT:** In Luke's gospel, we find out that one of the two rebels actually changes his mind and says, "Jesus, remember me when you come into your kingdom." Jesus replies, "Truly I tell you, today you will be with me in paradise" (Luke 23:42–43).

PRAY: Praise Jesus that He did not come down from the cross, but that He chose to save others instead of saving Himself. Praise Him that He is the King who came to serve. Pray for someone you love who doesn't trust in Jesus yet, that they would recognize who Jesus is and what He did for them on the cross.

JESUS DIES, THE CURTAIN TEARS, AND THE CENTURION SPEAKS.

When Jesus was baptized, Mark tells us that the heavens were "torn open" and a voice came from heaven saying, "You are my Son, whom I love; with you I am well pleased" (Mark 1:10–11). In our passage today, Jesus is crying out to God, the symbolic barrier between earth and heaven is being torn from top to bottom, and Jesus is declared to be God's Son.

Read Mark 15:33–41

What happened between noon and 3 p.m. while Jesus was being crucified (v. 33)?

⇒**SERIOUS FACT:** Darkness in the Bible is often a picture of God's judgment. For example, the prophet Amos writes, "'In that day,' declares the Sovereign Lord, 'I will make the sun go down at noon and darken the earth in broad daylight'" (Amos 8:9).

In verse 34, we get another snatch of Jesus speaking Aramaic. What did the prayer Jesus cried out mean in English (v. 34)?

Who did some people think Jesus was calling for when He said, "Eloi, Eloi" (v. 35)?

What did someone run to get and offer to Jesus (v. 36)?

What did this person say (v. 36)?

➡✦**IMPORTANT FACT:** Yesterday, we saw that Psalm 22 prophesies about people casting lots for Jesus' clothes. Psalm 22 begins: "My God, my God, why have you forsaken me?" (v. 1). On the cross, Jesus experienced God's judgment against our sin. Forsaken means abandoned. Jesus wasn't asking why God had forsaken Him as if He was surprised by the cross. God the Father, Son, and Spirit had always planned that Jesus would die like this. But Jesus cries out to God in His pain with words from the Old Testament to show how His death is fulfilling Old Testament prophecy.

➡✦**FUN FACT:** As we've already seen in Mark, lots of Jews believed that Elijah would come before the day of the Lord. There was also a tradition that Elijah would come to rescue righteous people who were in distress. The chief priests and teachers of the law sarcastically demand that Jesus prove He is the Messiah by coming down from the cross. This person seems like maybe he might *actually* be wondering if Elijah will come and help Jesus.

What does Jesus do in verse 37, and what happens to Him?

What happened to the curtain in the temple when Jesus died (v. 38)?

➡✦**FUN FACT:** In the temple, a thick curtain separated the Holy Place from the Most Holy Place, where God's presence was seen to dwell. Once a year, on the Day of Atonement, the high priest would go into the Most Holy Place on behalf of the people to sprinkle the blood of an animal sacrifice. When Jesus died, the real sacrifice was made and the curtain separating God's people from His presence was torn in two from top to bottom. Now, we can come to God through Jesus—not just once a year, but all the time!

How did the Roman centurion (which means a soldier who was in charge of a hundred other soldiers) react when he saw how Jesus died (v. 39)?

Mark's gospel starts like this: "The beginning of the good news about Jesus the Messiah, the Son of God" (Mark 1:1) Why is it shocking that the Roman centurion of all people said this about Jesus?

Which female disciples of Jesus were watching His crucifixion (v. 40)?

What does Mark tell us about these women (v. 41)?

PRAY: Praise Jesus that He took the judgment for our sin when He died on the cross and that His sacrifice has opened up the way for us to live with God forever. Pray that Jesus would help you follow Him for the rest of your life, knowing that you are loved and forgiven because of His death in your place.

JESUS IS BURIED

One day a few years ago, the three of us (Rebecca, Miranda, and Eliza) were driving past a cemetery. Eliza said, "Mummy, isn't that where all the dead people's bodies are rotting? That's gross." Rebecca replied, "Don't feel too superior to those dead people because you'll be dead one day as well, and your body will be rotting away. But if you've put your trust in Jesus, one day He will call you out of your grave and give you a resurrection body."

Read Mark 15:42–47

What day was it when Jesus died (v. 42)?

⇛✦**FUN FACT:** Instead of counting a day from midnight to midnight like we do, Jewish days ran from sundown to sundown. The Sabbath ran from sundown on Friday to sundown on Saturday. Jews were not allowed to work on the Sabbath, so time was running out that day for Jews to do any work.

What was the name of the man who came to Pilate as evening approached (v. 43)?

What does Mark tell us about Joseph of Arimathea (v. 43)?

✦*FUN FACT:* Joseph of Arimathea is a member of the Jewish Sanhedrin, which had condemned Jesus. John's gospel tells us that he is "a disciple of Jesus, but secretly because he feared the Jewish leaders" (John 19:38).

What did Joseph of Arimathea ask Pilate for (v. 43)?

What was Pilate surprised to hear (v. 44)?

What did Pilate do (v. 44)?

What did Pilate do when he'd had it confirmed that Jesus was dead (v. 45)?

✦*FUN FACT:* Jesus is on the cross for six hours before He dies. Most people who were crucified took longer than that to die. But the Roman centurion would have been a crucifixion expert, and he confirms that Jesus is dead.

What does Joseph of Arimathea do with Jesus' body (v. 46)?

How was Jesus' tomb closed up (v. 46)?

Who saw where Jesus' body had been laid (v. 47)?

_____

_____

_____

Look back at Mark 15:40. What do you notice about the women Mark names as witnesses of Jesus' death, and who he names as witnesses of Jesus' burial (v. 47)?

_____

_____

_____

⇻✦FUN FACT: In Jesus' day, women were not seen as reliable witnesses. But Mark names three women as witnesses of Jesus' crucifixion, and now he names two of them as witnesses of Jesus' burial. When the gospel authors give us names, they are usually pointing us to eyewitnesses whose testimony they are drawing from to write their biography of Jesus. Tomorrow, we'll see why Mark is mentioning these women in particular!

PRAY: Praise God that Jesus really did die and that His body was buried. Praise Jesus that that can give us hope today, even though we know that one day we will die and be buried as well.

JESUS COMES BACK TO LIFE—
IT'S WONDERFUL, TERRIFYING NEWS!

At the beginning of Act 6, we saw a woman who loved Jesus very much pouring ointment on His body. We read that Jesus said she had prepared His body for burial. In our final study today, we'll see three women coming to anoint Jesus' dead body but finding that it's not there anymore.

Read Mark 16:1–8

Who brought spices to anoint Jesus' body when the Sabbath was over (v. 1)?

Look back again at Mark's list of three women who witnessed Jesus' crucifixion (Mark 15:40). What do you notice?

What time of day was it when these women went to Jesus' tomb (v. 2)?

➡*FUN FACT:* This is the morning of the third day after Jesus was crucified. Jesus predicted three times that He would rise again on the third day (Mark 8:31; 9:31; 10:34).

What question did they ask themselves as they went (v. 3)?

_____

_____

_____

What did the women discover when they got to the tomb (v. 4)?

_____

_____

_____

When they went into Jesus' tomb, what did they see (v. 5)?

_____

_____

_____

How did they feel (v. 5)?

_____

_____

_____

➥**FUN FACT:** Matthew's gospel tells us that this man in white is an angel of the Lord and that he has rolled the stone away from Jesus' tomb (Matthew 28:2–3). John's gospel tells us there are two angels (John 20:12). This is not a contradiction, as the gospel authors often simplify their stories—just like you might tell your parents about a conversation you had with a friend at school and not mention another friend who was also in that conversation.

What does the angel tell the women about Jesus (v. 6)?

_____

_____

_____

What does the angel show the women (v. 6)?

Who does the angel send the women to talk to (v. 7)?

What message does the angel tell the women to give Peter and the others (v. 7)?

Why do you think the angel mentioned Peter in particular?

➡ *FUN FACT:* Mark's gospel is based on Peter's testimony, so we know Mark cannot mean here that the women didn't tell anyone at all. Instead, according to the other Gospels, the women did tell Peter and the rest of the disciples. But they didn't tell people in general what they'd seen. In the "Last Words" at the end of this study, we'll see that the women being afraid isn't evidence that they were cowards, but that they recognized how awe-inspiring Jesus' resurrection is! In Mark 14:9, Jesus said that wherever the gospel is proclaimed in all the world, the story of the woman who anointed Him for burial would be told in memory of her. At the end of Mark, the women who came to anoint Jesus' body for burial are remembered too.

How did the women respond (v. 8)?

PRAY: Praise Jesus that He came back from the dead, just like He said He would and that He's beaten death for us! Pray that He would give you courage to tell others about His life-saving death and amazing resurrection!

LAST WORDS

The ending of Mark's gospel feels sudden and weird. "Trembling and bewildered, the women went out and fled from the tomb. They said nothing to anyone because they were afraid" (Mark 16:8). But if we look back through Mark's gospel, we'll find that fear has been a regular response to Jesus' displays of power.

* It's the response of the disciples when Jesus proves His power over nature by calming a storm (Mark 4:39–41).

* It's the response of the people when Jesus proves His power over unclean spirits by throwing them into a herd of pigs (Mark 5:15).

* It's the response of the woman who had bled for twelve years when Jesus healed her and then asked, "Who touched me?" (Mark 5:33).

* It's the response of the disciples when Jesus walks toward them on the water (Mark 6:49–51).

* It's the response of Peter, James, and John when they see Jesus suddenly transfigured on a mountaintop and appearing with Moses and Elijah (Mark 9:2–6).

* It's the response of the disciples when Jesus predicts His death and resurrection for a second time (Mark 9:30–32).

Jesus is the Son of God. In the Old Testament, people knew they couldn't see God and live, so when God revealed Himself, they were completely terrified. Jesus is the most amazing hero. He's the Son of Man, who we'll see one day, coming on the clouds of heaven as the judge of all the earth. But He's also the most tender, gentle, loving human being ever to have lived.

* He's the one who touched a man with leprosy and made him clean (Mark 1:41).

- He's the one who welcomed little children, taking them in His arms and blessing them when His disciples thought that kids weren't worth His time (Mark 10:13–16).

- He's the one who recognized the bleeding woman who touched Him as His daughter and who took a dead twelve-year-old girl by the hand and told her in her native language, "Little girl, I say to you, arise" (Mark 5:41).

- And most importantly of all, He's the King who came not to be served, but to serve, and to give His life as a ransom for many (Mark 10:45).

We don't know how you feel about Jesus after reading through Mark's gospel. But hopefully, you've got a glimpse of both how loving and how terrifying Jesus is. Hopefully you've seen that He's the mighty King of all the world, but also the one who loves you so much He came to die so you could live.

The resurrected King of all the universe is reaching out in love to you today. If you've not yet repented and believed in Him, don't wait another minute. Throw yourself down at Jesus' feet, and He will lift you in His mighty arms and say to you, "Son, your sins are forgiven" (Mark 2:5) or "Daughter, your faith has healed you" (Mark 5:34).

If you have already put your trust in Jesus, thank Him for His power and His love today, and know He's got you safe in His arms whatever happens. Hear His words of resurrection life to you today: "For whoever wants to save their life will lose it, but whoever loses their life for me and for the gospel will save it" (Mark 8:35).

ACKNOWLEDGMENTS

We're so thankful to Trillia Newbell for suggesting we write this book, to Nathan Ridlehoover for reviewing it, and to Amanda Cleary Eastep and Avrie Roberts for editing it. We are grateful to Moody Publishers for letting us work as a team on this project, and we really hope you have enjoyed it!

—Rebecca, Miranda, and Eliza McLaughlin.